SpringerBriefs in Education

For further volumes:
http://www.springer.com/series/8914

Sharlene Chadwick

Impacts of Cyberbullying, Building Social and Emotional Resilience in Schools

 Springer

Sharlene Chadwick
North Ryde, NSW
Australia

ISSN 2211-1921   ISSN 2211-193X   (electronic)
ISBN 978-3-319-04030-1   ISBN 978-3-319-04031-8 (eBook)
DOI 10.1007/978-3-319-04031-8
Springer Cham Heidelberg New York Dordrecht London

Library of Congress Control Number: 2013956516

Printed on acid-free paper

Springer is part of Springer Science+Business Media (www.springer.com)

In the end we will remember not the words of our enemies, but the silence of our friends.

Martin Luther King Jr

For Jim
and
for Deb
who continue their unwavering love, support,
belief and friendship

Foreword

This is a very timely book about an important and contemporary topic—cyberbullying. The author presents the reader with an up-to-date overview of the key issues that can arise from young people's enthusiastic use of technology. When young people use technology not just to learn, communicate and express themselves but also to create risks to the well-being of others, they create challenges and dilemmas for schools that are not easily addressed.

The chapters in this book identify the features and impact of cyberbullying, outline the issues created by cyberbullying for schools and describe a range of educational approaches that have been used to address these challenges. In particular, they highlight the importance of prevention through education for cybersafety and helping young people to develop resilience.

Helen McGrath
RMIT University, Deakin University, School of Education

Preface

An integral part of how young people interact and live is increasingly evident in their online environment. Young people are exposed to imagery and behaviour they may not experience so early in their offline world. Cyberbullying is a recent phenomenon and presents challenges for researchers, schools, government policy makers, parents and the wider community. Cyberbullying is another form of bullying behaviour and not a separate issue in itself. Cyberbullying, like other forms of bullying behaviour, is about relationships, power and control. Cyberbullying at its core is 'relational' bullying and therefore requires a relationship management-based approach to dealing with its impacts and its prevention.

The focus on behaviour rather than the technology is paramount. Using language which focuses on behaviour as opposed to using words such as 'bully' or 'victim' is evident throughout this book. The term 'bully' implies that the issue is the individual. The term 'victim' has similar connotations, inferring helplessness. The interaction among the person, the situation and the technology is important.

There is no doubt that there are serious long-term effects of cyberbullying such as youth depression, anxiety, lower self-esteem and even suicide. However, the issue needs to be addressed within the broader social context and the development of a range of skills. Building social and emotional resilience in schools, and in young people themselves, will have a greater effect than regulation or legislation in dealing with cyberbullying. Teaching young people a range of social and emotional skills will assist them with cyberbullying. These include teaching pro-social values, emotional skills, social skills and high-order thinking skills. Promoting socially acceptable behaviour is effective.

Whole-school approaches and educating adults as well as young people is equally important. Effective policy is the backbone to good practice in schools and Internet safety should be no exception. Cybersafety is essential for all young people and needs to be embedded into the curriculum. Young people also need to, and want to, be involved in the development of materials or resources, they are part of the problem, they need to be part of the solution. Student-drive programs are effective in encouraging positive relationships and open discussions about what occurs online and offline. Young people are the experts with technology and often adopt a 'teaching' role for their parents and communication between school and home is important.

Cyberbullying crosses all domains and knows no geographical boundaries. It commonly occurs outside of school and can manifest itself 24/7. The ethical and legal issues regarding cyberbullying provide concern for teachers, schools and parents as there is limited clarity on the implications of cyberbullying.

Cyberbullying is a behavioural issue, not a technological problem. Initiatives and programs which focus on the enhancement of positive relationships and the developmental of behavioural skills are more effective in dealing with the impacts of cyberbullying.

Contents

Abbreviations

ABS	Australian Bureau of Statistics
ACBPS	Australian Covert Bullying Prevalence Study
ACMA	Australian Communications and Media Authority
AUCRA	Australian University Cyberbullying Research Alliance
CASEL	Collaborative for Academic, Social and Emotional Learning
ICT	Information Communications Technology
ISP	Internet Service Providers
ISTTF	Internet Safety Technical Task Force
NAPCAN	National Association for the Prevention of Child Abuse and Neglect
NSSF	National Safe Schools Framework
SEL	Social and Emotional Learning
SOSO	Smart Online Safe Offline

Chapter 1
Introduction

Abstract An integral part of how young people interact and live is increasingly evident in their online environment. This generation of young people are known as 'digital natives', they have not known a world where the use of technology is not present. As technology continues to embed itself within homes and schools, how young people use and access online environments is of interest to parents, government policy makers and the broader community. The implications to young people with this ease of access are significant. Cyberbullying is a recent phenomenon and presents challenges to both researchers and schools. Cyberbullying is another form of bullying behaviour and not a separate issue in itself. Cyberbullying, like other forms of bullying behaviour, is about relationships, power and control. However there is no common definition of cyberbullying and it takes many forms. The psychological and emotional impacts of cyberbullying on young people are similar to those of offline bullying behaviours. There are ways cyberbullying is significantly different from offline bullying.

Keywords Cyberbullying · Covert bullying · Offline bullying · Online environments · Harassment · Technology · Bystanders

1.1 Background

Over 20 years worldwide, bullying behaviours in schools have been a widespread issue, though the systematic study of the nature and prevalence of bullying behaviours in schools only began with the work of Olweus in the 1970s. The issue of bullying behaviours in Australian schools was recognised by the Australian House of Representatives Standing Committee on Violence in Schools, 1994, with the publication of *Sticks and Stones.*[1] The inquiry concluded bullying behaviours

---

[1] House of Representatives (1994).

S. Chadwick, *Impacts of Cyberbullying, Building Social and Emotional Resilience in Schools*, SpringerBriefs in Education,
DOI: 10.1007/978-3-319-04031-8_1, © The Author(s)

were becoming a major issue in Australian schools for students. The inquiry recommended the development of intervention programs to reduce bullying behaviours.

Cyberbullying is a recent phenomenon and presents challenges for both researchers and schools. It has been described as a new type of bullying behaviour with some different characteristics from offline bullying.[2] Limited research is available regarding the long-term effects cyberbullying can have on young people. However, research has suggested cyberbullying effects are similar to 'relational aggression' which is founded from a destructive relationship and intends to cause harm through humiliation, lying and depletion of social status and relationships.

The Australian Human Rights Commission recognises cyberbullying as a societal problem and therefore a human rights issue. In 2012 it launched a campaign BackMeUp to prevent cyberbullying at a national level. The aim of the campaign is to encourage young people to support their friends who may be targeted by cyberbullying.

Cyberbullying is another form of bullying behaviour and not a separate issue in itself. Cyberbullying, like other forms of bullying behaviour, is about relationships, power and control. Cyberbullying may be increasing with recent research suggesting 1:10 young people have been cyberbullied.

There is no doubt the nature of adolescent aggression has evolved due to the proliferation of technology and their access to information 24/7. As technology has evolved, cyberbullying has increased. The impacts of cyberbullying cannot be underestimated. Some cyberbullying can lead a young person to take their own lives. The destructive nature about 'words' or images online are they are publicly announced and often can only be changed or edited by the person who posted them. Young people who are the targets of cyberbullying stand out from their peers based on various factors including physical appearance, social skills, communication skills or their 'social status.'

The psychological and emotional impacts of cyberbullying on young people are similar to those of offline bullying behaviours. The difference is offline bullying usually stops when the school day ends. In cyberbullying there is no escape, technology follows young people into what was the safety of their own homes. Cyberbullying is more difficult for adults to detect or track and almost half of the young people do not know the identity of those who are engaging in cyberbullying.

1.1.1 Defining Cyberbullying

There is no commonly used or widely accepted standard definition of cyberbullying, which is considered to be a specific form of covert bullying. However progress toward which elements should be included in a definition has been made.

---

[2] Smith et al. (2008).

One of the ways in which a definition of cyberbullying is determined is to investigate the similarities and differences to offline bullying. The characteristics of power, repetition, intent and harm are all similar to traditional offline bullying.

Cyberbullying at its core is 'relational' bullying. The concept of 'repetition' is present in any type of bullying behaviour and is more evident in situations of cyberbullying. Usually one or more types of technology are used to engage in cyberbullying and are directed towards a specific person more than once. A single transmission of a defaming photo, message or personal information may bring about multiple responses from others, hence the term 'viral' when describing the reach of acts of cyberbullying.

According to Rigby (1996),[3] bullying can be defined as "repeated oppression, psychological or physical, of a less powerful person by a more powerful person or group of persons." This is the most frequently cited definition of offline bullying.

In 2007, the Kanderstag Declaration Against Bullying in Children and Youth[4] was developed. It states "bullying is a form of aggression, involving the abuse of power in relationships."

Belsey (2008b)[5] states "cyberbullying involves the use of information and communication technologies to support deliberate, repeated and hostile behaviour by an individual or group, that is intended to cause harm."

Smith et al. (2008)[6] define it as "an aggressive, intentional act carried out by a group or individual, using electronic forms of contact, repeatedly and over time against a victim who cannot easily defend him or herself."

In Australia, "cyberbullying appears to most commonly involve the malicious, targeted and repeated use of instant messaging and text messages with a trend towards the use of social networking sites by older students" Cross et al. (2009).[7]

Essentially, cyberbullying is an extension of bullying which may occur at school but the person doing the bullying uses new technology such as websites, text messages, social networking sites and emails to embarrass, demean, harass, intimidate, or threaten other people.

Cyberbullying could be defined as the use of technology to harass, threaten, embarrass, or target another person. Cyberbullying usually involves systematic communication over a period of time. It has many similarities with offline bullying however it differs in the person/people engaging in bullying behaviours can be, for the most part, anonymous. Cyberbullying is wide reaching and the material sent or uploaded can be difficult to remove.

It is useful to note, most young people who cyberbully also engage in bullying behaviours offline. Most students who are cyberbullied are also bullied offline.

---

[3] Rigby (1996).

[4] Kandersteg Declaration (2007).

[5] Belsey (2008b).

[6] Smith et al. (2008)

[7] Cross et al. (2009).

There is a need for an agreed definition of cyberbullying to assist Australian and international researchers. Many experts note it is difficult to define and when young people are asked to define cyberbullying they too find it difficult. Young people understand what constitutes cyberbullying however it's not a term they use, it tends to be an adult or media generated term.

1.1.2 Types of Cyberbullying

Cyberbullying can take many forms and is executed through online mediums including, but not limited to, email, chat rooms, and instant messaging on a website or via mobile phones. Anonymity is a key component to cyberbullying which means it is often difficult to determine the original source (Fig. 1.1).

Cyberbullying can be direct (overt) or (covert) and may include:

- direct harassment or intimidation;
- publication of malicious content;
- systems attack (hacking);
- manipulation of systems to exclude an individual; and
- false impersonation to misrepresent or defame.

Common types of cyberbullying behaviour can include:

- text based name calling;
- 'flaming' (overt attacks on a person), harassment or denigration;
- cyberstalking;
- using masquerade or exclusion;
- 'outing'; and
- sending or posting humiliating photos or videos and sharing videos of physical attacks on individuals.

The following explanations have been included to assist with understanding the complexities of the types of cyberbullying.

Harassment: Repeatedly sending offensive, rude, and insulting messages often sent at all times of the day and night. Some may even post their messages to public forums, chat rooms or a bulletin board where others can view the threats.

Denigration: Distributing information about another person which is derogatory and untrue through posting it on a Web page, sending it to others through email or instant messaging, or posting or sending digitally altered photos of someone.

Flaming: Online "fighting" or an intense argument using electronic messages in chat rooms, over instant messages or via email with angry, vulgar language. The use of capital letters, images and symbols add emotion to their argument.

Impersonation: Breaking into an email or social networking account and using that person's online identity to send or post vicious or embarrassing material to or about others.

Fig. 1.1 Cyberbullying (*Source* iStock) young people increasingly use technologies to engage in cyberbullying

Masquerading: Pretending to be someone else by creating fake email addresses or instant messaging names. They may also use someone else's email or mobile phone so it would appear as if the threats have been sent by someone else.

Pseudonyms: Using an alias or nickname online to keep their identity secret. Others online only know them by this pseudonym which may be harmless or derogatory.

Outing and Trickery: Public display or forwarding of personal communications such as text messages, emails or instant messaging. Sharing someone's secrets or embarrassing information, or tricking someone into revealing secrets or embarrassing information and forwarding it to others.

Cyber Stalking: This is a form of harassment. Repeatedly sending messages which include threats of harm or are highly intimidating, or engaging in other online activities which make a person afraid for his or her safety. Usually messages are sent through personal communications such as emails or text messages. Depending on the content of the message, it may also be illegal.

1.1.3 Online Environments

The web 2.0 world allows young people to create and share their content and express their ideas, thoughts and experiences on a worldwide stage. The online environment is generally delivered through internet platforms and covers a range of ways of informing and communicating with people. Online environments can be accessed virtually—anywhere, anytime and from many devices using any of these technological means. This access is from a wide variety of locations: home, work, school, libraries, public institutions and even coffee shops and stores.

The online environment has changed with the introduction of social networking sites, feeds and gaming consoles. Alternate media consumption of live streaming

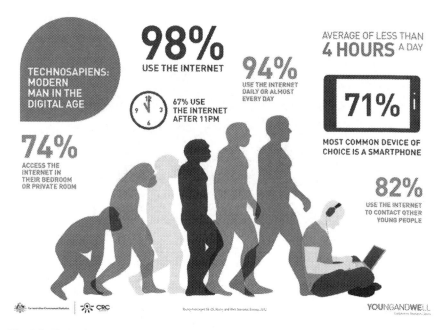

Fig. 1.2 Technology use in young Australians Young and Well CRC (2013).

and audio is changing the social interactions of young people. Pivotal innovations in online technologies have forever changed how young people interact. The internet and other platforms can now be accessed easily on smart phones, tablets, personal digital assistants; laptops have become smaller and lighter and 'notebooks' are highly portable.

Online environments are a valuable tool to bridge physical boundaries. In Australia there are more mobile phones than people and almost half the mobile phones have internet capability, one-third of users regularly access the internet on their phones (Fig. 1.2).

As technology continues to embed itself within homes and schools, how young people use and access online environments is of interest to parents, government policy makers and the broader community. The implications to young people with this ease of access are significant. The ability to monitor their online environments for adults is increasingly challenging. Parents/carers, teachers and anyone else who engages with young people need to become more informed and develop a greater understanding of online technology and its many uses. The online environment is constantly changing with new alternatives gaining ground with the release of the 'new' and 'latest' technology.

1.1.4 Access to Online Environments

Statistics from Australian Bureau of Statistics (ABS) (2011a) found:

- computers were available in more than 71 % households with 3–4 year olds; in 90 % of households with 7–8 year olds; and in almost all households with 8–17 year olds (98 %);
- internet access was available in more than 65 % of households with 3–4 year olds; increasing to more than 72 % of households with 7–8 year olds; and more than 90 % of households with 12–17 year olds;
- 84 % of 7–8 year olds sometimes used the internet at home to find information for school, send emails, chat online, surf the internet, play games or to access/ download music or movies;
- among 8–17 year olds, use of the internet for homework and leisure activities increased with age, from 61 % of 8–11 year olds to 83 % of 12–14 year olds and 88 % of 15–17 year olds;
- 74 % of parents of 7–8 year olds were comfortable with their child's media use.[8]

In 2009, the Australian Communications and Media Authority (ACMA) reported the internet is a regular part of everyday lives of children and young people aged 8–17 years and it is used regularly within both school and home environments.[9]

Australia now has a generation of young people who have never been without online access and who have integrated it fully into their lives. The current generation and those to come will be the most technologically literate generations and will only have ever known how to enhance relationships and learning in an online environment. They are often referred to as 'digital natives' or the 'digital generation' and have the ability to bypass physical access points which may have filters or other safety measures. Protection of young people online is challenging as education, research and the legal implications invariably lag behind the rapid evolution of technologies.

In 2009, 42 % of young people who used the internet at home reported they spent 2 h online per week; 17 % spent 3–4 h online; 21 % spent 5–9 h online and 13 % spent 10–19 h online.[10] Time spent online tends to increase with age with most young people spending an average of 30 min online per day.

Young people need to be in control of their own experiences in the online environment through education, knowledge and the development of skills.

---

[8] ABS (2011a).

[9] ACMA (2009).

[10] ABS (2011b).

1.1.5 Connections Between Online and Offline Bullying

The connection or nexus between online and offline bullying is evident. Online bullying is a new form of an old problem rather than a product of technology itself. Offline bullying has evolved into cyberbullying as technology progresses.

Cyberbullying allows the person anonymity without seeing the response or impact on the other person. The distancing effect often leads to young people saying or doing things which are more harmful than they would in a face-to-face situation. Both offline and online bullying behaviours are about relationships, power and control (Pepler 2007[11]; Belsey 2008a[12]) and research suggests young people who are bullied offline are also more likely to be bullied online.

There is an emerging trend to include both offline and online forms of bullying to maximise the impact upon the person. Offline name calling which involves face-to-face insults can spill over into online environments via instant messaging, text messages or email. Offline practical jokes as a means to humiliate someone are filmed or photographed and then posted or uploaded. Excluding young people from social events by not inviting them and then commenting about this on social networking sites or similar.

The reasons or motivations as to why young people engage in offline bullying are similar to those for online bullying.

1.1.6 Differences Between Online and Offline Bullying

There are ways cyberbullying is significantly different from offline bullying. One key difference is the perceived anonymity of technology. Young people report they will often use technology to 'say' things they would not normally say in a face-to-face conversation. This is also linked to a disinhibition related to the notion of anonymity. Young people have the ability to mask or withhold their identity online though the use of pseudonyms, impersonation, having multiple email addresses, using other mobile phones or having 'blocked' numbers.

Cyberbullying can occur at school, at home and out of school hours, therefore it can be more difficult to escape from cyberbullying. Smith et al. (2008)[13] found the occurrences of cyberbullying are not limited by time or place however most cyberbullying is enacted outside school hours. Students who are cyberbullied often experience no respite or refuge even in the comparative 'safety' of their own homes, Cross et al. (2009),[14] and this can lead to the potentially greater impacts cyberbullying has on young people as opposed to offline bullying.

---

[11] Pepler (2007).

[12] Besley (2008a).

[13] Smith et al. (2008).

[14] Cross et al. (2009).

Due to the use of technology to enact cyberbullying a wider audience is reached almost simultaneously of the act. It also has the potential to continue to enjoy a wider audience for an extended period of time. Messages, posts and images can be downloaded, saved, uploaded to other sites or forwarded to other people. In short, it is easier to 'share' cyberbullying. The public humiliation is greater and even if the posts or images have been removed or deleted, the digital footprint remains. The person being bullied never really knows when or where the post or image will reappear or be re-broadcast.

The role of the bystander is different in cyberbullying as it is more likely to occur when young people are either alone or amongst a wide range of friends and peers. If young people are alone they are less likely to have their friends or other people who can provide support available to them when cyberbullying occurs. In contrast sometimes the cyberbullying occurs in the presence of their friends who may provide tacit approval of the bullying behaviour. Some young people may become involved in cyberbullying by forwarding on messages or images without necessarily understanding the implications. Also due to the anonymous nature of cyberbullying some young people question whether it is a 'friend' engaging in the bullying behaviour particularly if messages are 'blocked' or received from a known address.

In a world of instant gratification there is a perceived 'glamorous' nature to cyberbullying. Many young people have skills in technology which far outweigh those of their parents or other adults including teachers and those of other young people. 'Bragging rights' may be common amongst young people, the notion of 'look at what I can do' which adds to the wealth of discussion regarding the presence of power in relation to bullying behaviours.

Bullying behaviours which have been enacted via technology are reported less often by young people. Cross et al. (2009)[15] found students who were cyberbullied were more reluctant to report to an adult as they perceive the consequences could include inaction, retaliation or removal of the use of technology. Belsey (2008b)[16] believes many young people fear an over-reaction from adults by banning them from access to technology. Young people's 'fear' of being socially isolated or excluded by being denied access to the use of technology may be viewed as greater than the 'fear' of the cyberbullying continuing.

Finally, adults can be less aware of cyberbullying as it tends to occur out of sight and in secret. Young people will often remove or delete messages or images before adults can view them. In addition, as it is difficult to define cyberbullying, adults are not sure whether what has occurred is in fact an instance of cyberbullying.

---

[15] Cross et al. (2009).

[16] Belsey (2008b).

References

Australian Bureau of Statistics. (2011a). *Household use of information technology.* Australia.
    Retrieved April 27, 2013, from http://www.abs.gov.au/ausstats/abs@.nsf/0/4E4D83E02F39F
    C32CA25796600152BF4?opendocument
Australian Bureau of Statistics. (2011b). *Australian social trends june 2011, children of the digital
    revolution, catalogue No 4102.0.* Retrieved April 28, 2013, from http://www.abs.gov.au/
    socialtrends
Australian Communication & Media Authority. (2009). *Generation M2: Media in the lives of
    8–18 year olds.* Retrieved April 28, 2013, from http://www.kff.org/entmedia/mh012010pkg.cfm
Belsey, B. (2008a). Retrieved May 5, 2013, from http://www.cyberbullying.org/
Belsey, B. (2008b). 'Cyberbullying: An emerging threat to the "always on" generation. *Canadian
    Teacher Magazine*, Spring *2008*, 18–20.
Cross, D., Shaw, T., Hearn, L., Epstein, M., Monks, H., Lester, L., & Thomas, L. (2009).
    *Australian covert bullying prevalence study (ACBPS), child health promotion research
    centre.* Perth: Edith Cowan University. Retrieved May 4, 2013, from www.deewr.gov.au/
    Schooling/NationalSafeSchools/Pages/research.aspx
House of Representatives Standing Committee on Employment & Education and Training.
    (1994). *Sticks and stones: Report on violence in Australian schools.* Canberra: Australian
    Government Publishing Service.
Kandersteg Declaration. (2007). *Against bullying and youth.* Retrieved April 10, 2013, from
    www.kanderstegdeclaration.com/storage/English%20KD.pdf
Pepler, D. & Craig,W. (2007). *Binoculars on bullying: A new solution to protect and connect
    children.* Retrieved April 28, 2013, from http://www.offordcentre.com/VoicesWebsite/library/
    reports/report-Feb2007-1.htm
Rigby, K. (1996). *Bullying in schools and what to do about it.* ACER: Melbourne. Retrieved
    April 10, 2013, from www.education.uinsa.edu.au/bullying
Smith, P. K., Mahdavi, J., Carvalho, M., Fisher, S., Russell, S., & Tippett, N. (2008).
    Cyberbullying: Its nature and impact on secondary school pupils. *Journal of Child Psychology
    and Psychiatry, 49*(4), 376–385.
Young & Well Cooperative Research Centre. (2013). Retrieved June 12, 2013, from https://
    www.facebook.com/yawcrc?fref=ts

Chapter 2
Cyberbullying

Abstract Young people's experience in the online environment is holistic. They use this environment to communicate, socialise, learn, research, complete homework and play. Their offline and online environments tend to blend into one which creates challenges in separating offline and online worlds for some young people. Cyberbullying amongst young people is more likely to occur outside of school hours however, the behaviours carry over from home to school and vice versa and can escalate quickly. Cyberbullying is a societal issue occurring in workplaces, families, institutions and any environment where power is misused and relationships are in conflict and requires a more complex relationship management based approach. The serious long term effects of cyberbullying, such as the higher prevalence of youth depression, anxiety and lower self-esteem, reinforce the need to address the issue effectively within a broad social context. Social media plays a role and young people need to be aware of the risks online and their digital footprint.

Keywords Cyberbullying · Young people · Prevalence · Forms of cyberbullying · Age and gender · Impacts of cyberbullying · Social media · Online risks · Digital footprint

2.1 The Online Environment for Young People

Most young people have regular access to online environments through home, school and even public libraries. Online environments are an important part of their education, social connections and recreation and they are the key 'users' in their engagement with the online world. Young people use the internet for an average of 1 h and 17 min each day.[1]

This equates to:

---

[1] McGrath (2009).

S. Chadwick, *Impacts of Cyberbullying, Building Social and Emotional Resilience in Schools*, SpringerBriefs in Education, DOI: 10.1007/978-3-319-04031-8_2, © The Author(s)

Fig. 2.1 Daily internet use
for young Australians

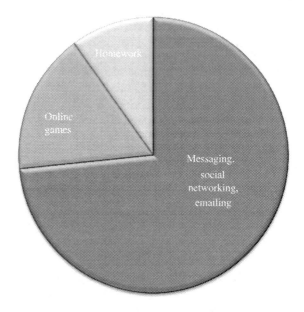

- almost 50 min of using the internet for messaging, visiting social websites and emailing;
- 15 min for online games with other players; and
- 13 min for homework.

Young people's capabilities within their online environment varies. Some young people have sound knowledge and skills which enable them to make good decisions regarding their online behaviour; some are more naïve and need education; some are more vulnerable and lack the social skills and resilience to cope with inappropriate encounters. Young people with mental health problems or disabilities are often vulnerable in the online environment. Young people identified as 'high-risk' in the offline world due to abuse or neglect are also 'high-risk' online. They are usually socially isolated and have experienced poor relationships with parents or other family members (Fig. 2.1).

The Australian Communications and Media Authority (ACMA) find more young people are becoming savvy online. They are increasingly aware of not disclosing names or passwords to others online yet cybersafety initiatives need to be continually promoted. However, many young people falsify their age online. Social networking sites require a minimum age of 13 though young people are able to change their dates of birth so they can join with limited verification. There are difficulties in verifying the age of young people online and some parents grant permission for their children to join these sites. The age requirement for social networking sites has been established for privacy reasons, websites are prohibited from collecting information on children younger than 13 years without parental permission. Falsifying age is becoming a common practice amongst young people and some parents. The message parents send by this practice is that lying is ok. There are some websites developed specifically for younger children which do not have an age restriction. Many young people have indicated they have 'chatted' with people online they don't know.

Young people's experience in the online environment is holistic. They use this environment to communicate, socialise, learn, research, complete homework and play. Their offline and online environments tend to blend into one which creates challenges in separating offline and online worlds for some young people. Due to this holistic approach, young people share a great deal of information about themselves online. For instance:

- name;
- age or birthday;
- address;
- telephone/mobile number;
- school attended;
- bank account details;
- holiday plans;
- passwords or email addresses; and
- photos.

This level of information is part of the 'identity mosaic' young people want to present to others. Young people want to strengthen offline relationships through online communications as well as seek out new online networks. ACMA's report, *Click and Connect,* found that purposeful divulgence of personal details was commonplace. Sometimes personal information was divulged without an understanding of the potential consequences of disclosure.[2]

Whist many adults are relatively new to the online environment and use it primarily for functions such as banking, shopping and emailing, young people use the online environment for different reasons. Pre-school aged children tend to visit children's websites, or those associated with their favourite show and email family members. Primary school aged children develop a growing confidence in visiting chat rooms and experimenting with search engines to download material. Adolescents are more independent and increasingly view online environments as social enablers. The age of the first use of the internet in Australia is at about 5 years old[3] with families of 6–10 year olds regularly involved in their internet access.

There are now approximately 2.2 million Australian children actively engaging online and the most common age group for entry into the online environment are 10–11 year olds.[4] The use of mobile phones and other wireless devices follows this early introduction and once in the online environment access through schools,

---

[2] ACMA (2009).

[3] ACMA (2007).

[4] McGrath (2009).

libraries and homes of friends will emerge. Some of this access will be unsupervised by an adult (Table 2.1).

2.1.1 Prevalence of Cyberbullying

Cyberbullying amongst young people is more likely to occur outside of school hours however, the behaviours carry over from home to school and vice versa and can escalate quickly. The most common place for cyberbullying to occur is at home followed by at school. It is recognised cyberbullying is not a problem isolated to schools. It is also a societal issue occurring in workplaces, families, institutions and any environment where power is misused and relationships are in conflict.

Limited research has been conducted into cyberbullying as it is a relatively new phenomenon though there are similarities between online bullying and offline bullying. An estimated 200 million children and young people globally are being bullied by their peers, according to the 2007 Kandersteg Declaration Against Bullying in Children and Youth. However, there is a lack of consistent and robust data on the prevalence of cyberbullying due to different assumptions leading to different methodologies. In addition without a common definition of cyberbullying there can be some confusion and ambiguity with survey questions. Reports in literature range from 4 to 42 % of all young people experiencing cyberbullying. Australian data suggests between 19 and 27 % are bullied at school and 10 % report being cyberbullied. Rates for cyberbullying are not as high as offline bullying though the widespread use of technology in recent years and experience from America and Britain suggests the increased potential for cyberbullying. The Australian University Cyberbullying Research Alliance (AUCRA) found rates of cyberbullying remained at under 22 % with females reporting higher rates than males.[5]

Under-reporting of cyberbullying by young people is evident. It is not reported to adults—teachers and parents—as often as offline forms of bullying behaviours, however, young people are more likely to speak with their parents than to teachers. Young people find it difficult to report cyberbullying because of the perceived shame associated with the incidents and the likelihood of reliving the experience. Young people are more likely to confide in their friends as much of the cyberbullying occurs without the knowledge of parents or teachers. In many studies females experience cyberbullying more frequently than males and most are reluctant to report. It is important to recognise who is engaging in the bullying behaviours: 46 % are other students; 34 % were friends; 16 % were siblings and about 1/3 did not know who it was Table 2.2.

---

[5] AUCRA (2010).

Table 2.1 Frequent online activities for 5–14 year olds[a]

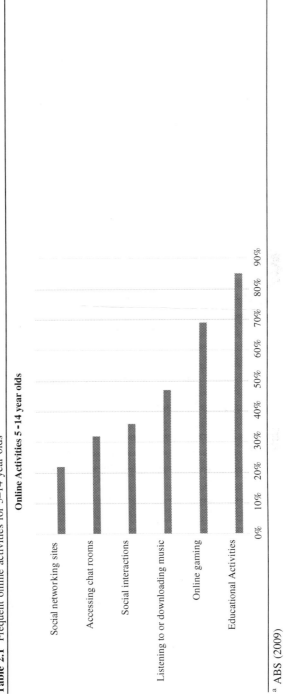

Online Activities 5-14 year olds

Table 2.2 Proportion (%) of those who have been targets of cyberbullying in past 12 months by age and gender[a]

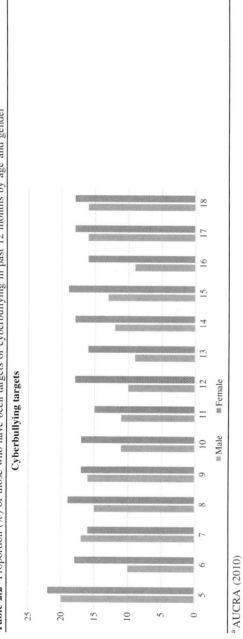

[a] AUCRA (2010)

An Australian study of covert bullying found there is also slightly higher rates of cyberbullying amongst secondary students and students from non-government schools.[6] Differences were also found in each age group regarding the mode of technology most prevalent for cyberbullying both within school and outside of school. This study also found cyberbullying is related to age and access to technology with older students more likely to engage in cyberbullying than younger students. The most common age to experience cyberbullying is during the transitional stages between primary and secondary schools then decreases towards the end of secondary school. Difficulties in forming positive relationships between school friends can lead to an increase in cyberbullying. Empathy for students who are being bullied decreases with age and if the student is male. This reflects data and research regarding offline bullying behaviours (Table 2.3).

The following international statistics are useful.

- nearly 43 % of young people have been bullied online
- 7–10 % of students are cyberbullied each term
- 70 % of students report seeing frequent online bullying
- over 80 % of young people use a mobile phone making it the most common medium
- 68 % of young people agree cyberbullying is a serious problem
- 81 % of young people think online bullying is easier to get away with than offline bullying
- 90 % of young people who have seen social networking bullying say they have ignored it
- 48 % of young people being cyberbullied do not report the incident
- 1:10 young people who are being bullied inform a parent or trusted adult
- girls are about twice as likely as boys to engage in, or be on the receiving end of, cyberbullying
- 58 % of children admit someone has said mean or hurtful things to them online
- 4:10 say it occurred more than once
- 75 % have visited a website 'bashing' another student
- young people who are cyberbullied are 2–9 times more likely to consider suicide
- hacking and cracking into social networking sites of others is high
- young people who bully have a one in four chance of having a criminal record by the age of 30
- bullying is the fourth most common reason young people seek help from children's help services

(Smith et al. 2008[7]; Hinduja and Patchin 2008[8]; Cross et al. 2009[9]).

---

[6] Cross et al. (2009).

[7] Smith et al. (2008).

[8] Hinduja and Patchin (2008).

[9] Cross et al. (2009).

Table 2.3 Common forms of cyberbullying

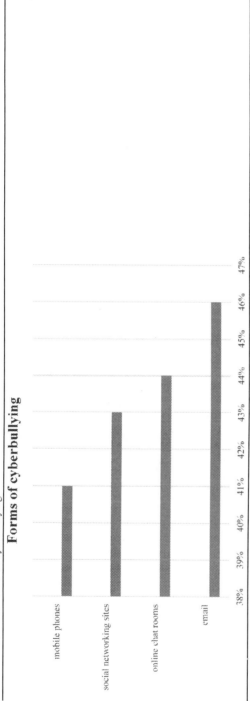

2.1.2 Gender Differences

There are gender patterns between females and males in regards to cyberbullying. Females prefer to engage in cyberbullying indirectly using relational means and are more likely to use the internet in order to attack their targets. Types of relational bullying or aggression include:

- gossiping;
- spreading rumours;
- friendship betrayal;
- excluding people; and
- other behaviours which manipulate relationships.[10]

Cyberbullying may be more prevalent than offline bullying however the focus on cyberbullying appears to be similar to the focus of offline bullying for females. The majority of cyberbullying is carried out by females and is consistent with the types of indirect bullying offline.

Females are often involved in cyberbullying as both target and those engaging in bullying behaviours. Females are more likely to be cyberbullied by text messages and phone calls than males[11] due to the relational aggression i.e. threats, blackmail, destroying friendships.[12] Females report when they do engage in cyberbullying they usually gossiped about or ignored someone. In the same study by Dehue et al. (2008), females reported being targets of cyberbullying more often via MSN, hacking or email. Stalking online also emerges as a common type of cyberbullying behaviour amongst females. In addition, females tend to be online more than males, for socialising purposes using emails, social networking sites and blogs more frequently than males. Female targets report problems such as harassment and threats being posted on their personal networking sites.

Male bullying more frequently involves physical altercations with fewer being the targets of online bullying than females. Males tend to spend more time online to play games[13] or watch movies etc. However, when males do engage in cyberbullying it is likely to involve posting hurtful pictures or videos (Table 2.4).

2.1.3 Impacts and Implications of Cyberbullying

The serious long term effects of cyberbullying, such as the higher prevalence of youth depression, anxiety and lower self-esteem, reinforce the need to address the issue effectively within a broad social context. The increased rate of poor mental

---

[10] Viljoen et al. (2005).
[11] Smith et al. (2008).
[12] Dehue et al. (2008).
[13] Dowell et al. (2009).

Table 2.4 Cyberbullying by gender[a]

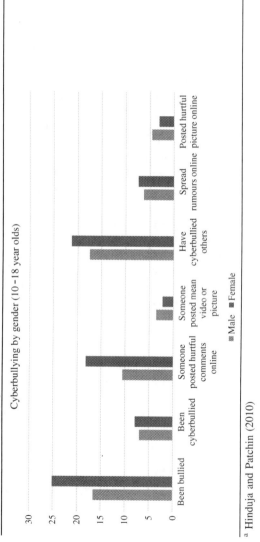

Cyberbullying by gender (10–18 year olds)

■ Male   ■ Female

[a] Hinduja and Patchin (2010)

health among young people has contributed to a wealth of programs designed to address a range of issues, particularly bullying behaviours. Cyberbullying is being recognised as an issue for workplaces, in relationships as well as in school communities. Society can no longer perpetuate the myth young people grow out of such behaviours. They need to be given the opportunity to be presented with a range of possible strategies from which they may choose an appropriate one for a particular situation.[14] Cyberbullying impacts upon both those engaging in the bullying behaviours and those on the receiving end.

Sawyer (cited in National Survey of Mental Health and Wellbeing 2000[15]) indicates 14 % of 4–17 year olds suffer from mental health problems. He also found rates of depression increased when relationships were poor, young people were less connected and young people were less involved. The British Medical Journal[16] published findings from an Australian study which demonstrated students who were bullied tended to be unhappy at school. However, these students enjoyed school but felt isolated and unsupported. This study also found students who bullied and were bullied had the greatest number of psychological and psychosomatic symptoms.

Cyberbullying rarely occurs in isolation, typically other students are aware of its occurrence. It is recognised bullying behaviours are fundamentally about relationship issues.[17] It is of critical importance students understand the significant role bystanders can play as their decision to become proactive can have a major influence in reducing cyberbullying within the school and even the wider community.

School culture also has a significant impact on cyberbullying. Cyberbullying can be entrenched in the culture of a school and the way in which teachers respond to offline and online bullying is imperative in dealing effectively with the issue. In some instances, the level of offline and online bullying behaviours perceived to occur in the school can impact upon its reputation. Schools need to continually build positive relationships with, and among, students and to give the issue constant attention.[18]

Research indicates there are long-term consequences for those who engage in persistent and systematic bullying behaviours. Lodge (2010)[19] posits an increase in juvenile anti-social behaviour such as vandalism, shoplifting and graffiti. Her research also demonstrated social and academic difficulties amongst students who frequently engage in bullying behaviours.

There is also a causal link between cyberbullying and depression, suicidal ideation and suicide attempts. It is increasingly clear any participation in bullying

---

[14] Hess et al. (2000).

[15] Sawyer (2000).

[16] British Medical Journal (1999).

[17] Pepler and Craig (2000).

[18] Chadwick (2010).

[19] Lodge (2010).

behaviours increases the risk of suicidal ideation and/or behaviours in a broad spectrum of youth.[20] The strongest association between involvement in bullying behaviours and depression, suicidal ideation and attempts can be found among those students who both engage in bullying behaviours and are being bullied.

Cyberbullying and victimisation have system-wide negative consequences. The natural tendency of a social group is to perpetuate itself. There are hidden influences in the peer group which encourage those who engage in cyberbullying to continue engaging in this behaviour and those who are being bullied to continue to be targeted.

Long-term consequences of cyberbullying are associated with perceived difficulties, hyperactivity, conduct problems, low pro-social behaviour, frequent smoking and drunkenness, psychosomatic symptoms i.e. headaches, stomach aches, and not feeling safe at school.[21] In addition students are more likely to engage in criminal activity as young adults, carry weapons and become violent outside of school and are involved in aggressive or abusive behaviour as adults.[22]

It can be suggested cyberbullying increases potential psychological consequences, such as loneliness, peer rejection, low self-esteem, poor mental health, depression, isolation, and hopelessness.[23] Whilst cyberbullying does not lead directly to suicide amongst young people there may be instances where the abuse is prolonged and systematic the person feels this is there only option. Peer harassment contributes to depression, decreased self-worth, hopelessness and loneliness—all of which are precursors to suicidal thoughts and behaviour.[24] Depression, hopelessness, and isolation have been linked to suicide. A phenomenon now being termed *cyberbullicide*[25] which is suicide directly or indirectly influenced by experiences with online bullying and aggression. These are isolated occurrences and do not reflect the norm however research by Hinduja and Patchin identified upward trends in 10–19 year olds. Cyberbullying victims were almost twice as likely to have attempted suicide compared to young people who had not experienced cyberbullying. Caution dictates many young people who have suicide ideation or commit suicide have often experienced other emotional and social issues in their lives. Cyberbullying could be viewed as the 'tipping point' for these young people.

Bullying behaviours, offline and online, impact on the climate of a school whether students are directly or indirectly involved. Peers serve as reinforcers and models of behaviour, and consequently classrooms containing high numbers of students with poor academic skills or behaviour problems are likely to promote these behaviours

---

[20] Kim and Levethal (2008).
[21] Sourander et al. (2010).
[22] Lodge (2010).
[23] Hinduja and Patchin (2010).
[24] Hinduja and Patchin (2010).
[25] Hinduja and Patchin (2010).

Table 2.5 Descriptors to describe how cyberbullying made young people feel[a]

Isolated	Vulnerable	Lonely
Excluded	Rejected	Powerless
Challenged	Bewildered	Depressed
Unsafe	Violated	Threatened

[a] Spears et al. (2008)

in individual students.[26] Poorer classroom environments were associated with poorer levels of student aggression, peer relations, and academic focus.

Students who are witnessing cyberbullying occurring can often feel anger, guilt, fear, powerlessness and sadness toward the student being bullied.[27] At times they can also experience the same negative feelings as those being bullied. Bystanders report a similar, if not greater, psychological impact as they believe the same behaviours could happen to them in the future.[28] Many students also feel guilty for not being able to intervene.

A culture within schools can also be created where bullying behaviours are accepted due to the feelings of powerlessness and isolation.[29] Research indicates some students believe cyberbullying could not be prevented in their schools. Students may consistently not attend school or have a desire to change schools.

Due to the covert nature of cyberbullying the impacts have the potential to be more severe psychologically, socially and emotionally. Cyberbullying magnifies offline bullying behaviours and affects mental, social and academic wellbeing of those being bullied. Short-term impacts include anxiety and depression, long-term impacts include health and social adjustment problems. Cyberbullying can also be malicious in content and the added complexity of not knowing the identity of those engaging in the behaviour increases the impacts on mental health issues for young people. The potential for humiliation in seeing posts or images online and being forwarded on and re-broadcast adds to the feelings of hopelessness and their perceived inability to escape from the 'attacks'. Emotional responses of young people vary from sadness to anger, frustration, and embarrassment to fear (Table 2.5).

2.1.4 Role of Social Media

The use of social media websites is the most common activity for young people worldwide though research on the impact of social media on young people is only recent. Any website which allows social interaction is a 'social media' site i.e.

---

[26] Barth et al. (2004).

[27] Batsche and Porter (2006).

[28] Rivers et al. (2009).

[29] Salmivalli and Voeten (2004).

social networking sites, gaming sites, virtual worlds, video sites and blogs. These sites have grown exponentially in recent years and provide a world of entertainment and communication for young people. However reality is becoming blurred between our offline and online worlds. A large proportion of this generations social and emotional development is occurring while online and through their mobile phones. This has led to increases in cyberbullying as well as privacy issues and other recent phenomena such as 'sexting' and internet addiction. Social media sites provide the forum for young people to participate online in the same way as they conduct their lives offline through connecting with friends and family, sharing photos and making new friends and expanding their networks.

Young people are also using social media to connect with others to complete homework and projects with some schools using blogs as teaching tools. Infographics are also becoming popular with the ability for young people to share and embed these within social media. Increased use of social media has been found to improve friendships and enables young people in remote areas to connect with others. For others it enables freedom of expression and engagement where face-to-face contact is limited.

Evidence is emerging social media provides a new way to promote social inclusion for young people. Many young people are marginalised or isolated because of their circumstances; however online social networking and digital media production can enable young people who are vulnerable to mental health difficulties to connect with others in meaningful ways which can positively affect their wellbeing. Most contact in the online world is with people they already know in the offline world and is used for both friendships and interest-based interactions. However, some young people do engage and interact with people they do not know in areas such as 'online communities' where there is an exchange of information or opinions on various topics. Within these 'communities' young people are interacting with others from different socio-economic backgrounds and different ages.

Emerging research in the field of digital technology use by young people and their communities at De Montfort University, UK[30] has identified a range of impacts on social capital and social cohesion resulting from the use of digital technologies by young people and their communities. Young people use social media extensively for collaboration and communication.

Today, 43 % of the world's population is 25 years old or younger. This young group is impatient and ready to change the world. Change for this generation has everything to do with people. Some 70 % of young people believe social media is a force for change.

---

[30] Boeck and Thomas (2010).

2.1.5 *Awareness of Online Risks*

Cyberbullying is not the only risk for young people online. The online environment presents some challenges for young people—peer-to-peer inappropriate content; lack of understanding of privacy issues; sharing too much information about themselves; posting false information about themselves or others; and outside influences by third-party advertising groups or potential predators.

There is also the risk of ownership of content posted online as many young people are becoming more concerned about who 'owns' their personal information online and in particular on social media. For some young people it is confronting to know some social media sites 'sell' private information to third-parties. There is a growing concern among young people in Australia of being targeted by advertising campaigns. In addition, the knowledge for young people that content posted such as personal information, opinions expressed and images cannot be deleted or removed permanently from the online environment.

Internet stranger danger appears to be over-exaggerated[31] though the potential danger does exist, the situation is a complex one and not as frightening as often portrayed. Young people are at more risk from someone they know or a family member than they are from an internet stranger. Studies by the Internet Safety Technical Task Force (ISTTF) found internet-related sex crimes are a small proportion of all sex crimes committed against young people. Internet predators are usually the same age or no more than 7 years older and have a tendency to use what is termed e-seduction rather than coercion. Young people who are drawn in by this usually display patterns of risk-taking behaviour offline and often agree to meet in person on the pretext of engaging in sexual activity.

Grooming refers to a range of behaviours which are calculated to enable an offender to procure a young person for sexual activity. Technology has not shown to increase the number of paedophiles though it has provided access to young people as personal information is easily found online. Most offenders who initiate sexual contact via the internet meet their targets in chat rooms[32] and this may be preceded by cyber-stalking. Research indicates 75 % of young people who meet the adult do so on more than one occasion and suggests the adult is using young people's natural curiosity towards sex and sexuality to build relationships—no matter how inappropriate.[33]

Photo sharing is another potential online risk for many reasons—privacy, ownership, inability to permanently remove or delete to name a few. Young people choose to post specific content online and photo sharing illustrates these risks. They could be exposing themselves or others to issues of permission, ownership and right of the individual to 'own' their personal information. There appears to be an absence of requiring or seeking permission to post a photo of someone else in a

---

[31] ISTTF (2008).

[32] Cross et al. (2009).

[33] Ybarra and Mitchell (2008).

public forum. Posting of specific content may also impact upon relationships when photos are either reposted or there is a request to remove the photo. At times when a relationship deteriorates the images may be posted online as a form of cyber-bullying Young people can learn a considerable amount from adults regarding the value of personal information and personal safety.

Linked to photo sharing is 'sexting'. This is a new risk to online activities and can be defined as sending, receiving or forwarding sexually explicit or suggestive messages, photographs or images via mobile phones or other digital devices. There is limited data available on how common this is amongst young people and might be due to young people not being willing to admit to this behaviour though it is becoming 'normalised behaviour' in adolescent culture. American research revealed 20 % of young people aged 13–19 have electronically sent or posted online nude or semi-nude images or videos of themselves—22 % female and 18 % male. 51 % of females in this age group said pressure from a male was the reason they sexted compared to just 18 % of males in this age group who said they felt pressure from a female.[34] At the same time, the risks to females are greater because generally, society judges girls and women far more harshly for sexual exhibitions than it judges boys and men.

However, young people refer to these self-portrait photos using a camera phone as 'selfies'. Selfies are commonly posted on social networking or photo sharing services. They are often casual, are typically taken either with a camera held at arm's length or in a mirror, and may include only the photographer or other people as well. Images of a sexually explicit nature which are saved, uploaded or for-warded have legal implications as it is by law distributing child pornography if the subject is under-age. This raises moral, ethical, legal and parenting concerns and more research is required to understand the motives for the behaviour. Concerns about criminal sanctions and complying with legislation need to be considered within the context of educating young people about the risks and the long-term consequences (Fig. 2.2).

Problematic Internet Use (PIU) was first described in the 1990s however there is no official recognition of PIU by authorities in most major countries. There may a predisposition in the media to promote internet addiction with limited validity. Excessive internet use is seen by some adults as a risk for many adolescents. Gaming is considered the major issue for many young boys as this is viewed as their social networking site. Young people may 'escape' their offline worlds by immersing themselves in their online world however, this should be addressed as a social issue rather than a technology issue. Whilst it is recognised some young people over-engage in the online environment there is no conclusive evidence to term this an 'addiction'.

Finally, identity theft can occur when personal information is obtained and used to obtain benefit. The fact many young people share or disclose information such as their date of birth, mobile phone numbers and other identifiers i.e. credit card

---

[34] National Campaign to Prevent Teen and Unplanned Pregnancy (2013).

Fig. 2.2 Percentage of young people by age who send nude or semi-nude images (Australia)

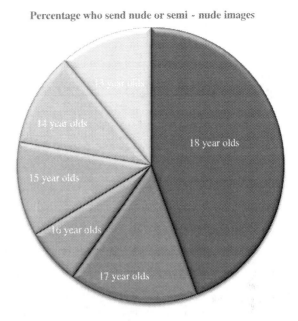

Percentage who send nude or semi - nude images

13 year olds
14 year olds
15 year olds
16 year olds
17 year olds
18 year olds

details or, passport numbers can lead to an increased risk of identity theft. Some young people also post and share personal information about their parents or siblings and thereby expose them to the risk of identity theft. Third-parties can use this information to obtain false or fake documents. However, many online documents have 'mandatory fields' and this presents further concerns as it's not possible to complete forms. Young people could also be more prone to cyberbullying with the level of detail others have regarding their personal information as social networking sites could be compromised or accessed without permission.

2.1.6 Digital Footprint

Every time an individual visits any website, they leave behind traces of which sites they have visited. This is commonly termed a 'digital footprint' and is an emerging threat to young people on social media. Our digital footprint can influence our reputations in future. Young people are not always aware that 'what goes online, stays online', the internet never forgets. Whilst images, posts and other messages can be 'deleted' or removed, there will *always* be a footprint. This may impact on future job or university prospects or alternately make young people more vulnerable to marketers or people wanting to defraud them. Many recruiters, employers and HR people have been known to reject a candidate based on information found online and in fact some insist an online search is undertaken for any candidate.

Our online image is equally as important as the image we present to people in our offline world. Disclosing more about ourselves online can actually decrease intimacy and satisfaction in our face-to-face relationships. Researchers are beginning to investigate how our online disclosures mirror who we are offline as more of our lives are being lived in both the physical and virtual worlds.

A fast growing industry is 'data mining', where a range of information is collected about an individual. Whilst primarily this is used for advertising and market research purposes, the footprint remains of every website, post, message or image.

References

Australian Bureau of Statistics (2009). *Household Use of Information Technology*, Australia. Retrieved April 27, 2013, from http://www.abs.gov.au/AUSSTATS/abs@.nsf/Lookup/4102.0Main+Features60Jun+2011

Australian Communications and Media Authority. (2007). *Internet Use and Social Networking by Young People No.1*. Retrieved May 31, 2013, from http://www.acma.gov.au/webwr/_assets/main/lib310665/no1_internet_use_social_networking_young_people.pdf.

Australian Communications and Media Authority. (2009). *Click and Connect: Young Australians' Use of Online Social Media—part 1*, (p. 8).

Australian University Cyberbullying Research Alliance (2010). *Submission to the Joint Select Committee on Cyberbullying-safety*, Prepared by Dr B Spears and Prof P. Slee. Retrieved June 10, 2013, from http://www.aphref.aph.gov.au_house_committee_jscc_subs_sub_62(1.)pdf

Barth, J. M., Dunlap, S. T., Dane, H., Lochman, J. E., & Wells, K. C. (2004, March-April). Classroom environment influences on aggression, peer relations and academic focus, *Journal of School Psychology, 42*(2), 115–133.

Batsche, G. M., & Porter, L. J. (2006). Bullying. In G. G. Bear & K. M. Minke (Eds.) *Children's Needs III: Development, Prevention, and Intervention* Bethesda, MD: National Association of School Psychologists, (pp. 135–148).

Boeck, T., & Thomas, J. (2010). *Amplified Leicester impact on social capital and cohesion.* United Kingdom: NESTA.

Chadwick, S. (2010). *They can't Hurt Me: A peer-led approach to bullying.* USA: VDM Publishing.

Cross, D., Shaw, T., Hearn, L., Epstein, M., Monks, H., Lester, L. et al. (2009). Australian Covert Bullying Prevalence Study (ACBPS), Child Health Promotion Research Centre, Edith Cowan University, Perth. Retrieved May 4, 2013, from www.deewr.gov.au/Schooling/NationalSafeSchools/Pages/research.aspx

Dehue, F., Bolman, C., & Vollnik, T. (2008). Cyberbullying: Youngsters' experiences and parental perception. *Cyberpsychol Behav, 11*, 217–223.

Dowell, E., Burgess, A., & Cavanaugh, D. (2009). Clustering of internet risk behaviour in a middle school student population. *Journal of School Health, 79*, 547–553.

Forero. R., McLellan, L., & Bauman, A. (1999). Bullying behaviour and psychological health among school students in NSW, Australia: cross-sectional study. *British Medical Journal.*

Hess, H., Senecal, S., Kirouac, G., Herrera, P., Philippot, P., & Kleck, R. E. (2000). Emotional expressivity in men and women: Stereotypes and self-perceptions. *Cognition and Emotion, 14*(5), 609–642.

Hinduja, S., & Patchin, J. (2008). Cyberbullying: An exploratory analysis of factors related to offending and victimisation. *Defiant Behaviour, 29*(2), 1–29.

Hinduja, S., & Patchin, J. W. (2010). Bullying, cyberbullying, and suicide. *Archives of Suicide Research, 14*(3), 206–221.

ISTTF. (2008). *Enhancing Child Safety and Online Technologies: Final Reports of the Internet Safety Technical Task Force to the Multi-State Working Group on Social Networking of State Attorneys General of the United States.* The Berkman Centre for Internet and Society, Harvard University. Retrieved June 14, 2013, from http://cyber.law.harvard.edu/research/isttf

Kim, Y. S., & Levethal, B. (2008). Bullying and suicide: A review. *International Journal of Adolescent Health. April–June 2008, 20*(2), 133–154.

Lodge, J. (2010). *The bully/victim continuum: Stability of peer victimisation in school and patterns of Internalising and externalising problems in early adulthood.* Paper presented at the Eleventh Australian Institute of Family Studies Conference, Melbourne, July 7–9, 2010.

McGrath, H. (2009). *Young People and Technology. A review of the current literature* (2nd ed.). Melbourne: The Alannah and Madeline Foundation.

National Survey of Mental Health and Well-being. (2000). Retrieved April 10, 2013, from www.mja.com.au/public/issues/186-04-190207/saw10752.fm.html

Pepler, D., & Craig, W. (2000). Making a Difference in Bullying. Retrieved June 12, 2013, from http://www.melissainstitute.org/documents/MakingADifference.pdf

Rivers, I., Poteat, V. P., Noret, N., & Ashurst, N. (2009). Observing bullying at school: The mental health implications of witness status. *School Psychology Quarterly, 24*(4), 211.

Salmivalli, C., & Voeten, M. (2004). Connections between attitudes, group norms, and behaviour in bullying situations. *International Journal of Behavioural Development, 28*(3), 246–258.

Sex and Tech. (2013). *Results from a survey of teens and young adults.* The National Campaign to Prevent Teen and Unplanned Pregnancy. Retrieved June 22, 2013, from http://www.ikeepsafe.org/be-a-pro/relationships/whats-wrong-with-sexting/

Smith, P. K., Mahdavi, J., Carvalho, M., Fisher, S., Russell, S., & Tippett, N. (2008). Cyberbullying: Its nature and impact on secondary school pupils. *Journal of Child Psychology and Psychiatry, 49*(4), 376–85.

Sourander, A., Brunstein Klomek, A., Ikonen, M., Lindroos, J., Luntamo T., Koskelainen, M., et al. (2010). Psychosocial risk factors associated with cyberbullying among adolescents: a population-based study. *Archives of General Psychiatry, 67*, 720–728.

Spears, B., Slee, P., Owens, L., and Johnson, B. (2008). *Behind the Scenes: Insights Into the Human Dimension of Covert Bullying.* Retrieved June 13, 2013, from http://foi.deewr.gov.au/system/files/doc/other/behind_the_scenes_-_insights_into_the_human_dimension_of_covert_bullying_-_final_short_report.pdf

Viljoen, J. L., O'Neill, M. L., & Sidhu, A. (2005). Bullying behaviours in female and male adolescent offenders: Prevalence, types and association with psychosocial adjustment. *Aggressive Behavior, 31*, 521–536.

Ybarra, M., & Mitchell, K. (2008). How risky are social networking sites? A comparison of places online where youth sexual solicitation and harassment occurs. *Pediatrics, 121*, 355.

Chapter 3
Social and Emotional Resilience

Abstract Young people undergo continual changes affecting all aspects of their lives—social, cognitive, emotional and physical. The transition into young adulthood may present challenges for some and the need to develop social and emotional resilience to cope with these is crucial. Social and emotional wellbeing refers to the way a person thinks and feels about themselves and others. It includes being able to adapt and deal with daily challenges, which incorporate the need to be resilient and have a range of coping skills, while living a life of purpose and fulfilment. An emphasis on the behavioural and emotional strengths of young people, as well as how they respond to adversity or challenging situations. These competencies provide resilience against stressors of cyberbullying and help to prevent behavioural and emotional difficulties developing later in life. Research has found building social and emotional resilience in children and young people is crucial in dealing with cyberbullying. It is commonly viewed that protective factors assist in building resilience. Young people need to be taught coping strategies early as they immerse themselves in the online world. They are exposed to imagery and behaviour they may not experience so early in the offline world therefore building resilience in children and young people strengthens their ability to cope with negative online experiences such as cyberbullying.

Keywords Resilience · Social and emotional wellbeing · Social competence · Emotional competence · Protective factors · Peer victimisation · Role in bullying · Risk factors · Mental wellbeing

3.1 Resilience Research and Background

Researchers such as Michael Rutter, Norman Garmezy, Emmy Werner and Anne Masten pioneered developmental longitudinal studies in resilience. The construct of resilience emerged accidentally from longitudinal studies of children at risk and this prompted a paradigm shift from studying risk factors to investigating

S. Chadwick, *Impacts of Cyberbullying, Building Social and Emotional Resilience in Schools*, SpringerBriefs in Education,
DOI: 10.1007/978-3-319-04031-8_3, © The Author(s)

protective factors. There is evidence social competence is a predictor of life success and empathy is also one of the most critical competencies for social and cognitive development. However, our knowledge of resilience is constantly evolving.

Michael Rutter—a psychiatrist, describes protective factors and protective mechanisms and discusses the difference between these. He offered a critical bridge between resilience research and practice. Prevention involves both the environment and the individual in dynamic interaction—this is the protective process.

Norman Garmezy—a researcher, explored childhood competence by studying children who were succeeding in spite of overwhelming odds. He studied the forces assisting children to survive and adapt. His studies over 50 years consistently conclude resilience plays a significant role in the mental wellbeing of young people.

Emmy Werner—a child psychologist, conducted a 40 year study which began in 1955, of children at risk as they developed throughout their life. This study lead to the emergence of resilience as a protective factor to recover from, and overcome, problems. In this study 1:3 of these children grew into competent young adults by 18 and most of the others had settled down by the time they reached 32.

Anne Masten—a child psychologist, found resilience among children was not necessarily an extraordinary feat but a combination of skills, resources and support from others which revealed the power of the 'ordinary'. She posits children require nurturing and some do not have adequate protective factors nor the opportunities or experiences which nurture resilience.

By the 1990s most research confirmed resilience was an interactive process occurring between individuals and their environment. Intervention to assist young people to develop resilience can occur at any number of places and in a variety of ways. Resilience is attributional and contextual—a dynamic inner and outer process. The notion of resilience emphasises we can assist young people to identify, develop and access protective factors to minimise the potential damage of stressors and develop resilience.

We all know what resilience means until we try to define it. There are many different definitions of resilience but all refer to the capacity of the individual to overcome adversity. It includes social competence, problem solving skills, critical consciousness, autonomy and a sense of purpose. There are several definitions of resilience though it is commonly referred to as the ability to 'bounce back'. Masten et al.[1] define resilience as "the process of, capacity for, or outcome of, successful adaptation despite challenging or threatening circumstances."

Fuller[2] describes resilience as "the happy knack of bungy jumping through the pitfalls of life." Grotberg[3] states "resilience is the universal capacity which allows

[1] Masten et al. (1990).

[2] Fuller (1998).

[3] Grotberg (1995).

a person, group or community to prevent, minimise or overcome the damaging effects of adversity." Ungar[4] says resilience is the "capacity of individuals to navigate their physical and social ecologies to provide resources, as well as their access to families and communities who can culturally navigate for them."

Resilience has often centered on the individual coping styles of stress, problem solving, and facing adversity without disintegration and discussed as that aspect of mental health and coping which is paramount to the ability to spring back during adverse circumstances. The mention of positive health is linked to the ability to withstand and cope with stress adaptively. Resilience refers to overall physical and psychological health, and has been described as the ability to "bounce back from adversity.[5]"

3.1.1 Social and Emotional Wellbeing

The study of social and emotional wellbeing is a holistic concept and still a new phenomenon though many of the concepts defined under the broader notion of social and emotional wellbeing have been studied for decades. Social and emotional wellbeing can be viewed as the absence of mental health disorders however, it encompasses much more than this.

Social and emotional wellbeing refers to the way a person thinks and feels about themselves and others. It includes being able to adapt and deal with daily challenges, which incorporate the need to be resilient and have a range of coping skills, while living a life of purpose and fulfilment. An emphasis on the behavioural and emotional strengths of young people, as well as how they respond to adversity or challenging situations. Many of the characteristics of social and emotional wellbeing follow a developmental pathway, and age-appropriateness is therefore a key factor in measurement.

Social and emotional wellbeing incorporates the environments such as families and schools as well as the individual characteristics of the person. A wide range of terminology is used to describe social and emotional wellbeing which include social and emotional 'competence', 'intelligence', 'development', 'learning' or 'literacy'. The domains of social and emotional wellbeing which are evident are:

- Individual—internal (intrapersonal) and relational (social/interpersonal) characteristics; and
- environmental—family/home; early education settings/school and community. The effect of these varies according to the age of the child/young person.

Socially and emotionally competent young people have good relationships with others, are confident, can communicate well, do better at school, take on and

---

[4] Ungar (2008).

[5] Reivich et al. (2011).

persist with challenging tasks, have a sense of mastery and self-worth and develop the peer and adult relationships necessary to succeed in life. Such competencies may provide resilience against stressors and help to prevent behavioural and emotional difficulties developing later in life.

3.1.1.1 Social Competence

Social competence is defined by personal attributes such as cooperative and pro-social behaviour, helpfulness, the ability to initiate and maintain positive relationships and resolve conflict. Factors affecting how young people form and maintain social relationships with their families, peers and teachers include attachment, conflict resolution, social and interpersonal skills. Some young people may face more difficulties in their social relationships than others; the ability to deal with these depends on their personal attributes and the social supports or networks they have. Socially competent young people are able to develop the peer and adult relationships needed to succeed in both academic and non-academic environments. Socially competent young people demonstrate more positive school behaviours and fewer mental health problems.

3.1.1.2 Emotional Competence

Emotional competence is the extent to which one is aware of, and able to act on, one's own and others' emotions, as well as the ability to regulate emotional experience within oneself (intrapersonal) and to be effective in interactions with others (interpersonal).[6]

Emotional regulation is the monitoring, evaluation and modification of emotional reactions (both positive and negative) in a socially appropriate manner. Its development is particularly important as it can influence other personal attributes and affect how children think about and interact with their world.

Conflict in interactions with others is an unavoidable part of life from time to time. How young people adjust to or deal with conflict, and the extent to which they are affected by or able to cope effectively with daily problems, are determined partly by their emotional security and regulation and partly by the level of social support they have.

3.1.2 Protective Factors

The paradigm shift to focus on protective factors has been brought about by the social and cultural changes young people now face:

---

[6] Humphrey et al. (2010).

- cyberbullying;
- childhood and youth depression;
- youth suicide;
- media exposure to negative aspects of life;
- media images of physical, emotional, economic and social issues;
- high societal and cultural diversity;
- changing family structures;
- changes in parenting;
- fast pace of change;
- high levels of boredom; and
- high levels of youth unemployment.

Discussions relating to resilience are usually framed within risk, vulnerability and protective factors. It is the complex relationship between these influences which can determine the outcomes for young people. Newman[7] reviewed these influences:

- risk—any factor or combination of factors which increases the chance of an undesirable outcome affecting a person;
- vulnerability—a feature which renders a person more susceptible to threat;
- protective factors—the circumstances which moderate the effects of risk; and
- resilience—positive adaptation in the face of severe adversities.

Resilience strengths are viewed as developmental and are provided through external supports and opportunities which are developed in the right environment. They can be classified into four key areas (Table 3.1):

- social competence;
- problem solving;
- autonomy; and
- sense of purpose.

In 1993–1994 an International Resilience Project[8] was conducted involving 30 countries where children have faced extreme adversity. Grotberg summarised the findings and noted resilience is internal and people exhibit a number of features which assist them in viewing circumstances more optimistically. To overcome adversities, children draw from three sources of resilience features labelled: I have, I am, I can (Fig. 3.1).

What children and young people draw from each of the three sources may be described as follows (Table 3.2).

A resilient child does not need all of these features to be resilient, but one is not enough. A child may be loved (I have), but if they have no inner strength (I am) or social, interpersonal skills (I can), there can be no resilience. A child may have a great deal of self-esteem (I am), but if they do not know how to communicate with

---

[7] Newman (2004).

[8] Grotberg (1995).

Table 3.1 Developmental factors for resilience

Social competence	Problem solving	Autonomy	Sense of purpose

• Responsiveness
• Communication
• Empathy/caring
• Compassion/
  altruism
• Forgiveness
	• Planning
	• Flexibility
	• Resourcefulness
	• Critical thinking
	• Insight
		• Positive identity
		• Internal locus of control
		• Initiative
		• Self-efficacy
		• Mastery
		• Adaptive distancing/
		  resistance
		• Self-awareness
		• Mindfulness
		• Humour
			• Goal direction
			• Achievement
			• Motivation
			• Educational
			  aspirations
			• Special interest
			• Creativity
			  imagination
			• Optimism
			• Hope
			• Faith
			• Spirituality
			• Sense of meaning

Fig. 3.1 I have, I am, I can model

Table 3.2 I have, I am, I can attributes

I have	I am	I can

• Trusting relationships
• Structure and rules
• Role models
• Encouragement to be autonomous
• Access to health, education,
  welfare and security systems
	• Loveable and my
	  temperament is
	  appealing
	• Loving, empathic and
	  altruistic
	• Proud of my
	  achievements
	• Autonomous and
	  responsible
	• Filled with faith, hope and
	  trust
		• Communicate
		• Problem solve
		• Manage my feelings and
		  impulses
		• Gauge the temperament of
		  myself and others
		• Seek trusting relationships

Table 3.3 Determinants of resilience

Tension	Explanation
Access to material resources	Availability of financial, education, medical and employment assistance and/or opportunities as well as access to food, clothing and shelter
Relationships	Relationships with significant others, peers, adults and within ones family and community
Identity	Personal and collective sense of purpose, self-appraisal of strengths and weaknesses, aspirations, beliefs and values, spiritual and religious identification
Power and control	Experiences of caring for one's self and others; the ability to effect changes in one's social and physical environment in order to access health resources
Cultural adherence	Adherence to one's local and/or global cultural practices, values and beliefs
Social justice	Experiences related to finding a meaningful role in the community and social equality
Cohesion	Balancing one's personal interests with a sense of responsibility to the greater good; feeling part of something larger than oneself, socially and spiritually

others or solve problems (I can), and has no one to help them (I have), the child is not resilient. A child may be very verbal and speak well (I can), but if they have no empathy (I am) or does not learn from role models (I have), there is no resilience. Resilience results from a combination of these features.

Ungar[9] describes tensions both within and around the individual to enable them to thrive and survive. The balance of these tensions determines the resilience of the individual (Table 3.3).

Fuller[10] conducted qualitative research with young people in Victoria, Australia to determine factors and characteristics which enabled them to 'bounce back'. He categorised these as protective factors which enable young people to develop resilience during tough times (Table 3.4).

Supportive relationships protect young people from stress and strengthen resilience. Positive, long-lasting relationships early in life are the strongest predictor of success later in life. Protective factors will vary according to the needs and circumstances young people face. Student group protective factors are important in adolescence when young people are exploring their own identities, worth and values. They seek affirmation from those who they admire and with whom they feel a connection. Others have categorised protective factors to include aspects such as:

- positive self-perception—strong sense of self-efficacy;
- coping skills—to deal with stressful situations;

---

[9] Ungar (2008).

[10] Fuller (1998).

Table 3.4 Protective factors

Level	Protective factor
Community	• Culture of cooperation • Stability and connection • Good relationships with adults outside the family • Opportunities for meaningful contribution
School	• Sense of belonging and fitting in • Positive achievements an evaluation at school • Having someone outside your family who believes in you • Attendance at a pre-school
Family	• Sense of belonging and connectedness to family • Feeling loved and respected • Proactive problem solving and minimal conflict during infancy • Maintenance of family rituals • Warm relationship with at least one parent • Absence of divorce during adolescence • 'Good fit' between parents and child
Individual/peers	• Temperament, activity level, social responsivity, autonomy • Developed a special talent, curiosity or zest for life • Work success during adolescence • High intelligence

- positive sense of identity—fundamental to mental wellbeing; and
- sense of personal choice—responsibility for feelings and actions.

A useful framework is to describe resilience in terms of intrinsic and extrinsic factors.

Intrinsic factors are:

- Secure base—sense of belonging and security;
- Self-esteem—internal sense of self-worth and competence; and
- Self-efficacy—mastery, control and understanding personal strengths and limitations.

Extrinsic factors are:

- at least one secure attachment relationship;
- access to wider supports such as extended family and friends; and
- positive school and/or community experiences.

All of these act as a reference point for building social and emotional resilience in young people. Emotional resilience, the ability to draw on personal strengths to cope with stress, is critical in assisting young people to deal with cyberbullying. Resilient young people have the ability to adapt to, handle and overcome difficult situations. Although many resilient young people may have some biological inclination toward being more resilient, researchers have found it can be learned. However, being resilient does not mean young people will not experience difficulty or upset. It is natural to feel emotional pain and sadness when being cyberbullied. The learning is how young people deal with the emotional pain. When young

Fig. 3.2 Domains of
resilience

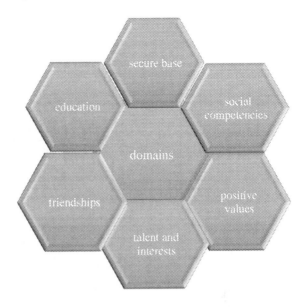

people are resilient, they cope with cyberbullying much more effectively than those
who are not resilient (Fig. 3.2).

3.1.3 Social and Emotional Resilience and Cyberbullying

Research has found building social and emotional resilience in children and young
people is crucial in dealing with cyberbullying. It is commonly viewed protective
factors assist in building resilience. Young people need to be taught coping
strategies early as they immerse themselves in the online world. They are exposed
to imagery and behaviour they may not experience so early in the offline world
therefore building resilience in children and young people strengthens their ability
to cope with negative online experiences such as cyberbullying. The ability to
'bounce back' may assist young people to be less vulnerable and minimise the
impact of negative comments, postings or images online. Ensuring young people
are resilient when using technology can begin with (Fig. 3.3):

- being empathic to the world young people live in;
- communicating effectively and active listening;
- develop responsibility in online behaviour; and
- actively encourage young people to have time away from technology.

Providing young people with a solid foundation of emotional resilience enables
them to have the ability to adapt to and overcome the challenging situations they
may encounter online. Some simple ways for parents to build resilience in children
and young people is to:

Fig. 3.3 Using technology.
(*Source*: iStock) Parents are
encouraged to monitor and
teach young people how to
use technology appropriately

Ensure they feel accepted. When children feel accepted for who they are, they
are more able to cope with stress and adversity. They need to know parents believe
in them and like who they are. Additionally, when they feel accepted at home the
issues with cyberbullying are less debilitating.

Nurture a positive self-view. Teach your children to see value in what they
have to offer the world around them. Also, help them see themselves in a positive
light, especially during difficult times. And allow them to see the challenges from
cyberbullying are not a reflection of who they are but instead are choices made by
others.

Encourage positive emotions. Encourage children to find pleasure and humour
in life. Provide opportunities for children to relax with fewer schedules and
commitments.

Manage feelings. Children need to learn how to calm down when they feel like
they are falling apart emotionally or when they are feeling aggressive and angry.
Help children learn to recognise and name their feelings and reactions. Providing
suggestions on how to manage those feelings in positive ways.

Promote problem-solving skills. One way to instill problem-solving skills is to
demonstrate how to be flexible in responding. Discuss the pros and cons of different options and allow children to choose the best course of action for themselves
at that point in time.

Orient towards the future. Children need to know there is a future beyond this
current situation. The key is not to keep focusing on the negative aspects of
cyberbullying and to see there are other things in life including things to look
forward to and work toward. Positive thinking enables children to see the good
things in life and keep going even in the most challenging situations.

Challenge any self-critical behaviours. When children have a critical inner
voice, it's important this type of thinking is challenged. Allowing children to
believe self-criticisms can lead to any number of long-term impacts. Instead, teach
them how to identify negative thoughts and overcome this way of thinking.

Encourage new challenges. Children should be encouraged to experience new
activities, especially if they are challenging. Finding a balance between leaving

them to figure it out alone and overprotecting them is important. Children who are overprotected learn helplessness.

Address problems immediately. Ignoring the fact children are struggling or dealing with cyberbullying does not build resilience, it creates feelings of isolation.

Discourage avoidance. Children should be encouraged to talk about painful events. When children talk about the negative impacts of cyberbullying it assists them to make sense of the experiences.

Reframe negative experiences. Encourage children to keep perspective of the cyberbullying by reframing the situation so they can learn from it. The more children talk about being a victim, the worse they feel.

Look for self-discovery opportunities. When children are faced with a difficult situation, this also can be a very good time to learn something about who they are. For instance, your child may find they have a lot of self-control or situations are easier to navigate when they ask for help. Children who are able to turn a negative situation of cyberbullying into an opportunity to learn are more resilient.

Role model. It is no longer enough to simply tell children how to behave in certain situations, we need to demonstrate how to cope and deal with difficult situations.

In any situation where bullying is occurring either offline or online, young people choose to take on one of three roles: the bystander, the person engaging in bullying and the person being bullied. Bullying rarely occurs in isolation, typically taking place in the presence of other students. It is recognised bullying behaviours are fundamentally about relationship issues. The social nature of bullying behaviours has led to a focus on research of the role of bystanders and the degree of influence which they can exert in the situation. It is of critical importance young people understand the significant role bystanders can play as their decision to become proactive can have a major influence in reducing bullying behaviours both in the offline and online worlds (Fig. 3.4).

The **person engaging in bullying** may be doing so to gain social status, and bullying has probably proven to be a successful strategy in gaining that status.

The **person being bullied** is attempting to avoid the hurt and stop the situation.

The **bystander** faces discomfort with what they are witnessing and faces the challenge of deciding how to respond.

With each of these roles, there is a choice of responses. Developing emotional resilience is about teaching young people strategies to enable them to make better choices which will assist them in resolving a bullying situation successfully, whether it is offline or online. Young people do not always have the skills to negotiate complex social situations such as cyberbullying successfully. Young people need to be given the opportunity to be presented with a range of possible strategies from which they may choose an appropriate one for a particular situation. In addition, young people need to learn how to deal with these challenging situations without resorting to 'mean' behaviours. Essentially they need to learn how to advocate for themselves as well as others.

Fig. 3.4 Interrelationship
between roles in bullying

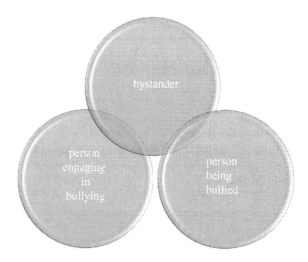

In the same way learning to write does not just happen for children, similarly, learning to interact socially occurs when young people learn the skills, are guided and are provided the opportunities to practise. Human beings are social beings and we need to learn how to empathise, share and negotiate. Many young people are not provided the chance to learn these skills because adults intervene and solve problems for them. Unstructured play time, when children had the opportunity to work out their disagreements, has been replaced by organised activities, usually coordinated by adults, or online games.

The increased awareness of cyberbullying provides an opportunity to teach the skills of resilience and to negotiate and manage social challenges successfully. These are also considered to be life-long skills and can be transferred to a range of contexts other than cyberbullying.

Resilience is our response to challenging situations and how we demonstrate coping strategies. The choices we make need to leave us feeling good about ourselves and others, maintains integrity and is probably one of the most important lessons young people need.

Social support or connections with others have a positive effect on the well-being of young people. They provide the social relationships which act as buffers from stress and challenging situations increasing a sense of belonging, purpose and self-worth. Young people who feel connected to others and groups are less likely to be negatively impacted upon by cyberbullying.

3.1.4 Peer Victimisation

Cyberbullying has damaging effects on the mental and physical wellbeing of young people. Some researchers have suggested peer victimisation is an outcome of bullying behaviours and others frame the phenomenon more broadly. There is evidence to suggest the prevalence of peer victimisation is greater amongst younger students and most bullying is found to occur in school and involves verbal aggression with boys being significantly more likely to be bullied than girls. Victimisation tends to decrease in successive years of primary schooling and increases when students enter the first year of secondary school.

There is also a causal link between peer victimisation and low self-esteem, high levels of social alienation, poorer psychological functioning and poorer self-image and poor school adjustment. In addition higher levels of depression, poor general health, social isolation and suicidal thoughts have also been attributed to systematic and prolonged peer victimisation. Interpersonal correlates such as rejection, lack of friends and low friendship quality is also attributed to peer victimisation. Peer rejection in the early school years is linked to social exclusion and peer victimisation. Children who are withdrawn or who demonstrate aggressive behaviour are at greater risk of being excluded and thereby subjected to bullying behaviours.

There is a causal link between peer victimisation and internalising behaviours such as school avoidance, low academic achievement and lack of school enjoyment. Other studies have found increased levels of psychosomatic symptoms among victimised students—headaches, stomach cramps, coughs, and sore throats are present some three years later. This suggests increased stress levels associated with prolonged victimisation has a direct impact on physical health.

Peers are important in understanding victimisation and bullying. 80–90 % of peers report it is unpleasant to watch bullying occurring in their school[11] though they are drawn into bullying interactions by arousal and excitement of aggression. Peers have also been observed adopting a range of roles: reinforcers, assistants, defenders or outsiders.[12] There is evidence to suggest bullying and victimisation have negative influences on the group as well as individual students. The phrases 'social theatre' and 'social architecture' have emerged to explain how student roles actually encourage bullying behaviours. Pro-social controllers demonstrate positive characteristics (e.g. positive social skills), intrinsic friendship motivations and positive wellbeing.

Friendships and supportive family relationships are powerful protective factors against the negative influences of peer victimisation. Changes in students' friendships can be related to changes in social adjustment. Victimisation influences a students' view of others and there is evidence of a risk for social maladjustment. Young people who are rejected or socially isolated are at higher risk for developing behavioural and emotional disorders (Table 3.5).

Young people reporting cyberbullying varies as it is dependent on how cyberbullying is defined and the age of those surveyed. A study conducted by

---

[11] Pepler and Craig (2000).

[12] Salmivalli (2007).

Table 3.5 Victimisation and cyberbullying offences[a]

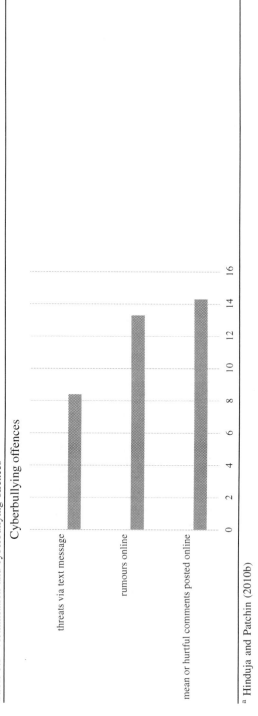

Cyberbullying offences

[a] Hinduja and Patchin (2010b)

Hinduja and Patchin in the USA found an average of 27 % of young people between the ages of 11–18 have been cyberbullied.[13]

The type of technology used to victimise others is also important. Mobile phones are most commonly used followed by social networking sites. Cyberbullying and victimisation vary according to gender as well with females reporting a higher percent than males. However, males may be reluctant to report a cyberbullying incident or a past bullying experience.

Some young people who are victimised engage in deviant behaviour and possibly delinquency. Victimised people have a tendency towards anti-social behaviours in an attempt to find a release for the negative emotions they might be feeling. There are long-term consequences for those who engage in persistent and systematic bullying behaviours. An increase in juvenile anti-social behaviour such as vandalism, shoplifting and graffiti has been found and social and academic difficulties amongst students who frequently engage in bullying behaviours, both offline and online.

There is also a causal link between bullying behaviour and depression, suicidal ideation and suicide attempts. It is increasingly clear any participation in bullying behaviours increases the risk of suicidal ideation and/or behaviours in a broad spectrum of youth.[14] The strongest association between involvement in cyberbullying and depression, suicidal ideation and attempts can be found among those students who both engage in cyberbullying and are being cyberbullied.

Bullying and victimisation have system-wide negative consequences. The natural tendency of a social group is to perpetuate itself. There are hidden influences in the peer group which encourage those who engage in cyberbullying to continue engaging in this behaviour and those who are being bullied to continue to be targeted.

Long-term consequences of cyberbullying are associated with perceived difficulties, hyperactivity, conduct problems, low pro-social behaviour, frequent smoking and drunkenness, psychosomatic symptoms i.e. headaches, stomach aches, and not feeling safe at school.[15] In addition students are more likely to engage in criminal activity as young adults, carry weapons and become violent outside of school, and are involved in aggressive or abusive behaviour as adults.

It can be suggested cyberbullying increases potential psychological consequences, such as loneliness, peer rejection, low self-esteem, poor mental health, depression, isolation, and hopelessness. Depression, hopelessness, and isolation have been linked to suicide.

---

[13] Hinduja and Patchin (2010a).

[14] Kim and Levethal (2008).

[15] Sourander et al. (2010).

3.1.5 Social and Emotional Learning

Parents and educators want young people to have the motivation and ability to achieve academic success, establish positive relationships with their peers and adults, adapt to the developmental changes, contribute to their friendship group, family and wider community and to make informed decisions to enhance their mental, social and emotional wellbeing. This in turn may assist in the reduction of anti-social behaviours such as cyberbullying as a connection to school decreases the prevalence of these behaviours.

Many young people lack social-emotional competencies and social and emotional learning (SEL) provides a systematic way for them to develop and enhance skills and become more connected. Key skills of empathy, decision making and conflict resolution are important to this end. SEL provides the opportunity for young people to recognise and manage their emotions, appreciate the perspectives of others, develop pro-social behaviours and use a variety of interpersonal skills to effectively deal with difficulties. These are essential in dealing with cyberbullying.

A body of research is emerging which investigates the impact on behaviour and school performance through the implementation of SEL programs[16] as a way forward to enhance young people's success at school and in their community. SEL is the process through which young people acquire the knowledge, attitudes and skills to:

- recognise and manage emotions;
- set and achieve positive goals;
- demonstrate care and concern for others;
- establish and maintain positive relationships;
- make responsible decisions; and
- handle interpersonal situations effectively.[17]

The environments developed through SEL support and reinforce positive behaviours and encourage young people to practise skills in their offline and online interactions. The development and maintenance of positive relationships assist in decreasing the impact of cyberbullying.

The Collaborative for Academic, Social and Emotional Learning (CASEL) have identified features which are crucial to the development of social and emotional competencies (Fig. 3.5).

- **Self-awareness**—accurately assessing one's feelings, interests, values, and strengths/abilities, and maintaining a well-grounded sense of self-confidence.
- **Self-management**—regulating one's emotions to handle stress, control impulses, and persevere in overcoming obstacles; setting personal and academic goals and then monitoring one's progress toward achieving them; and expressing emotions constructively.

---

[16] Durlak et al. (2011).

[17] Durlak and Weissberg (2010).

Fig. 3.5 Cognitive, affective and behavioural competencies

- **Social awareness**—taking the perspective of and empathising with others; recognising and appreciating individual and group similarities and differences; identifying and following societal standards of conduct; and recognising and using family, school, and community resources.
- **Relationship skills**—establishing and maintaining healthy and rewarding relationships based on cooperation; resisting inappropriate social pressure; preventing, managing, and resolving interpersonal conflict; and seeking help when needed.
- **Responsible decision-making**—making decisions based on consideration of ethical standards, safety concerns, appropriate standards of conduct, respect for others, and likely consequences of various actions; applying decision-making skills to academic and social situations; and contributing to the wellbeing of one's school and community.[18]

They involve firstly instruction in processing, integrating and selectively applying social and emotional skills in developmentally, contextually and culturally appropriate ways. Secondly, SEL programs foster young peoples' social-emotional development through the establishing of safe, caring learning environments involving peers, improved classroom management and teaching practices, and whole-school approaches (as cited in Durlak et al.).

Young people need to learn to identify and regulate their feelings (i.e. differentiating between anger and sadness). Awareness of feelings enables young people to identify the physical state and thoughts associated with those feelings which in

---

[18] CASEL (2009)

turn assists them in developing a constructive sense of self. The ability to moderate negative feelings and control impulsive actions and behaviours are important in relation to cyberbullying (i.e. not posting a comment or image in response for being angry or upset). These are also important in developing self-confidence and resilience. The social situations and interactions young people experience, whether offline or online, extend their awareness and understanding of feelings and attributes to others. This is the basis of being empathic—the ability to recognise the feelings of others and take on their perspective.

Positive attitudes and values which guide and influence behaviour is another competency for SEL. These focus on the intentions which drive the behaviour and are important in gaining an understanding as to why some people engage in cyberbullying. Personal responsibility, empathy, respecting others and social responsibility are also key factors in assisting young people to make effective decisions using a range of solutions for varying situations (i.e. choosing not to forward a post or image).

Social interaction skills are critical in individuals being able to follow through with the decisions they have made. Young people need the ability to effectively communicate—verbally and non-verbally—to clearly express their thoughts and feelings. Often the way young people communicate online is misinterpreted because the nuances and intent are unclear. The fact 'emoticons' and text speak such as 'LOL' have been developed and widely used indicates the intent of the message can be misinterpreted.

SEL also develops skills in negotiating resolutions for conflict, cooperating with others, refusing to participate in irresponsible behaviours and increasing the help-seeking capacity of young people. Young people may feel more comfortable and confident in approaching an adult to report cyberbullying. These skills need to be constantly and positively reinforced.

A focus on the social, emotional and even moral climate in which young people interact may prevent and lead to a reduction in bullying behaviours. The social and emotional competence of the entire school community will also have an impact on the level of bullying behaviours. Existing research suggests universal school-based prevention programs (i.e. those developed for all children and young people in the school context) can be effective. A report by the Task Force on Community Preventive Services[19] determined universal school-based programs were effective in reducing or preventing violent and aggressive behaviour among children and young people. Key factors of these programs included topics and skill development such as:

- emotional self-awareness;
- emotional control;
- empathy;
- self-esteem;
- positive social skills;

---

[19] Hahn et al. (2007).

- social problem solving;
- conflict resolution; and
- team work.

A review of school-based interventions[20] designed to prevent bullying behaviours found the most effective interventions use a whole-school universal approach consisting of multi-faceted elements.

- school-wide rules and sanctions;
- teacher training;
- classroom curricula;
- peer mediation, ethics classes or circles;
- conflict resolution training; and
- individual counselling.

Programs directed solely at the person engaging in bullying behaviours, the target or both, without involving and including other students or addressing the larger school climate issues are less likely to be effective. Successfully addressing both online and offline bullying behaviours requires the whole-school community promoting a culture of respect. Expectations for how staff, students and parents treat one another and interact should be reflected in school policies, classroom rules and consistently modelled and reinforced by all adults in the school context.

Implementation of any program or intervention is often a challenge in school settings. Farrington et al.[21] in their meta-analysis of 59 different anti-bullying programs determined the most successful interventions included a variety of elements. The following elements comprise a whole-school approach:

- whole-school anti-bullying policy;
- school conferences/assemblies providing information about bullying to students;
- curriculum materials;
- classroom management and classroom rules;
- cooperative group work among experts (e.g. teachers, counsellors and interns);
- work with bullies, work with targets, work with peers (e.g. peer mediation, peer mentoring, peer group pressure as bystanders);
- information for teachers and parents;
- improved playground supervision;
- disciplinary methods;
- non-punitive methods (e.g. Pikas, No Blame);
- restorative justice approaches (e.g. ethics classes, circles);
- school tribunals, school bully courts;
- teacher training and professional development; and
- parent training/meetings.

---

[20] Vreeman and Carroll (2007).
[21] Farrington and Ttofi (2009).

Reductions in bullying behaviours were seen to be greater in schools where a whole-school approach is adopted and the extent to which programs and interventions are implemented. It is difficult to state the type of program which is more successful in reducing bullying behaviours as there are several common elements in a range of programs implemented, however the duration and intensity was found to be important. Programs need to be intensive and long-lasting to have an impact and to build the culture which effectively and proactively deals with offline and online bullying behaviours. In addition the size of classes and the quality and accessibility of training for teachers is also seen as key to effective implementation of any anti-bullying intervention.

Programs which use multiple procedures are more likely to be effective in reducing bullying behaviours. These include:

- educational programs—improving teacher awareness and understanding of the phenomena of cyberbullying;
- cyberbullying policies—supported by the whole-school community including teachers, students and parents;
- curriculum material—raise awareness of cyberbullying among students, acquisition of pro-social values and skills, acceptance of differences, assertiveness, proactive behaviour for bystanders; and
- procedures for dealing with cyberbullying.

3.1.6 Mental Wellbeing

The mental health and wellbeing of young people is a major concern in many countries. Mental health is a state of wellbeing in which every individual realises their potential, can cope with the normal stresses of life, can work productively and is able to make a contribution to their community.[22]

The Australian National Mental Health Plan 2009–2014 has a priority area for prevention and early intervention which states a clear action for work with schools to deliver programs to improve mental health literacy and enhance resilience.[23] A range of strategies, programs and mental health promotion activities can be implemented at a school level to address behaviours such as cyberbullying. These programs need to be consistent in their approach. Schools are important environments for improving mental health literacy and developing skills in resilience and coping.

Social isolation or rejection at school are linked to a range of issues and can decrease mental health and wellbeing.[24] In Australia, programs such as *KidsMatter* and *MindMatters* and the *beyondblue* initiative have had a significant impact on

---

[22] WHO (2011).

[23] National Mental Health Plan (2009–2014), Commonwealth of Australia (2009).

[24] McGrath and Noble (2010).

mental health promotion. In addition there are a range of other programs in place in schools which address mental health and wellbeing, social and emotional resilience and cyberbullying.

3.1.6.1 Indicators for Mental Health

Researchers highlight the significance of protective factors in contributing to an individual's ability to demonstrate resilience. Resilience can be enhanced through explicit instruction involving a range of coping strategies. Indicators of good mental health among young people may include:

- feeling connected to their school;
- having positive family—school links;
- feeling connected to peers;
- feeling cared for and supported by teachers;
- having a sense of belonging and worth;
- having one caring adult outside the family;
- being involved in community life;
- knowing how to think optimistically;
- having skills for being resilient;
- demonstrating competence in social skills; and
- being emotionally literate.

3.1.6.2 Mental Health Statistics

Anxiety disorders are the most common mental health problems experienced by young people. In Australia, anxiety disorders are estimated to affect about one in every 10 young people aged 18–24 years,[25] with the rates higher among young females (14 %) compared to males (8 %). Young people experience mental health problems at higher rates than older age groups and retain their increased risk beyond youth into older age.[26] Over a quarter of all young Australians aged 16–24 experience a mental health disorder. The most common anxiety disorders reported by young Australians are social anxiety and post-traumatic stress disorder.

Evidence continues to accumulate regarding child and adolescent mental health problems in Australia.

---

[25] HeadSpace (2013).
[26] Eckersley (2007).

3.1.6.3 Kids Helpline (2011)

- 19 % of all counselling sessions nationally related to emotional wellbeing, which was the major issue for young people
- 10 most viewed hot topics for children—bullying (2244), young people—cyber bullying (10297) and parents—cyberbullying (16664)
- one in four young people receive professional help
- boys are more likely to experience mental health problems than girls
- 1:5 adolescents with mental health problems reported suicidal ideation.[27]

3.1.6.4 Social and Emotional Wellbeing Survey (SEWB) (2007)

- four in 10 students worry too much
- three in 10 students are very nervous/stressed
- two in 10 students have felt hopeless and depressed for a week and have stopped regular activities
- One third of students lose their temper a lot and sometimes engage in bullying behaviours
- Two-thirds of students are not achieving as well in their schoolwork as they could
- four in 10 students have difficulty calming down (poor resilience)
- social and emotional health decreases from primary to secondary school.[28]

3.1.6.5 National Survey of Mental Health and Wellbeing (2000)

- 14 % of 4–17 year olds suffer from mental health problems
- young people with mental health problems experience problems in most areas of their life
- rates of depression increase for young people when:
- their relationships are poor
- they are less connected
- they are less involved.
- anxiety and depression are the most common mental health problems for young people aged 12–17
- school-based programs support young people with mental health problems.[29]

---

[27] Kids Helpline Overview (2011).

[28] ASG (2007).

[29] Sawyer et al. (2001).

Table 3.6 Risk factors in mental health

Individual	• Poor social skills
	• Low self-esteem
	• Body concept
	• Poor diet
	• Inadequate sleep
Family or social	• Social isolation
	• Marital discord
	• Stress relating to family conflict
	• Parental mental disorder
School context	• Bullying and cyberbullying
	• Peer rejection
	• Failure to achieve
	• Inadequate behaviour management
Life events and situations	• Abuse and neglect
	• Physical illness
	• Family breakdown
	• Abandonment or loss
Community and cultural	• Socio-economic
	• Social or cultural discrimination
	• Housing conditions

3.1.6.6 Determinants

There are a range of risk factors which are associated with the development of mental health problems in young people. Different risk factors may be closely associated with one another. A diverse range of social, environmental, biological and psychological factors can impact on an individual's mental health. In turn, people can develop symptoms and behaviours which are distressing and interfere with their social functioning and capacity to negotiate daily life (Table 3.6).

The harm inflicted by cyberbullying has long-lasting implications and can result in mental wellbeing issues and negative impacts for years to come. Many young people deny or play down the emotional harm caused by cyberbullying though research suggests differently. Studies demonstrate up to 38 % felt vengeful; 37 % were angry and 24 % felt helpless.[30] Females are more emotionally affected by cyberbullying than males. Females are more likely to report being frustrated, angry and sad than males. Anger and frustration tend to be the primary emotional impact among young people. Younger children who do not report cyberbullying or who internalise the hurt and upset are likely to have mental wellbeing issues with serious implications as the rate of emotional distress is higher.

Young people now navigate their relationships both online and offline. Information Communication Technology (ICT) plays a significant role in the lives of young people, yet the current evidence-base supporting its role in mental health

---

[30] Hinduja and Patchin (2009).

promotion activities is not well established. Wyn et al.[31] outlined four key gaps in the available literature:

- **Wellbeing**—there is a lack of comprehensive and systematic research on the nature and meaning of relationships and social connections and the role they play in enhancing (or harming) young people's health and wellbeing.
- **Meaning and social context**—little research in the complexity of internet use.
- **Diversity**—gaps exist in research on the experiences of young people from a variety of backgrounds.
- **Participant research**—the opportunity exists to involve young people in the design and implementation of research.

ICT is an integral part of daily life for many young Australians and can promote social inclusion and access to resources and information. The online environment can serve to connect those young people who have difficulties with face-to-face interactions and relationships.

References

Australian Schloarships Group Student Social and Emotional Health Report. (2007). Reteieved July 6, 2013, from http://www.asg.com.au/Assets/Files/ASG_State_Student_Social_Emo_Health_short[2].pdf

CASEL. (2009). Social and emotional learning and bullying preventation. Retrieved October 7, 2013, from, http://casel.org/wp-content/uploads/SEL-and-Bullying-Prevention-2009.pdf

Commonwealth of Australia. (2009). Fourth National Mental Health Plan—an agenda for collaborative government action in mental health 2009–2014, ACT.

Durlak, J.A., & Weissberg, R.P (2010). *Better evidence-based education: Social and emotional learning.* Retrieved June 29, 2013, from www.casel.org/publications/social-and-emotional-learning-programmes-that-work

Durlak, J.A., Weissberg, R.P., Dymnicki. A.B., Taylor, R.D. Schellinger, K.B. (2011, January/February). The Impact of enhancing students' social and emotional learning: A meta-analysis of school-based universal interventions. *Child Development, 82*(1), 405–432.

Eckersley, R. (2007). The health and wellbeing of young australians: present patterns and future challenges. *International Journal of Adolescent Medicine and Health, 19*(3), 217–227.

Farrington, D.P., & Ttofi, M.M. (2009). *School-based Programs to Reduce Bullying and Victimization,* Campbell Systematic Reviews, Cambridge University, Cambridge, UK.

Fuller, A. (1998). The Resilience Project, Protective Factors. Retrieved June 29, 2013, from http://www.sofweb.vic.edu.au/edlibrary/public/stuman/wellbeing/MindYouthpdf

Grotberg, E. (1995). International Resilience Project. Retrieved June 29, 2013, from http://resilnet.uiuc.edu/library/grotb95b.html

Hahn, R., Fuqua-Whitley, D., Wethington, H., Lowy, J., Liberman, A., Crosby, A., et al. (2007). The effectiveness of universal school-based programs for the prevention of violent and aggressive behavior: A report of recommendations of the Task Force on Community Preventive Services. *Morbidity and Mortality Weekly Report, 56*(RR07), 1–12.

HeadSpace—what works, research and information. Retrieved July 6, 2013, from http://www.headspace.org.au/what-works/research-information/anxiety

---

[31] Wyn et al. (2005).

Hinduja, S., & Patchin, J.W. (2009). *Cyberbullying: Emotional and psychological consequences.* Cyberbullying Research Centre.

Hinduja, S., & Patchin, J. W. (2010a). *Lifetime cyberbullying victimization rates.* Cyberbullying Research Centre. Retrieved July 6, 2013, from http://www.cyberbullying.us/2010_charts/cyberbullying_victimization_meta_chart.jpg

Hinduja, S., & Patchin, J.W. (2010b). *Cyberbullying Victimisation.* Cyberbullying Research Centre. Retrieved July 6, 2013, http://www.cyberbullying.us/2010_charts/cyberbullying_offending_meta_chart.jpg

Humphrey, N., Kalambouka, A., Wigelsworth, M., Lendrum, A., Lennie, C., & Farrell, P. (2010). New beginnings: Evaluation of a short social–emotional intervention for primary-aged children. *Educational Psychology, 30*(5), 513–532.

Kids Helpline Overview. (2011). Retrieved July 6, 2013, from http://www.kidshelp.com.au/upload/22918.pdf

Kim, Y.S., & Levethal, B. (2008). Bullying and suicide: A review. *International Journal of Adolescent Health, 20*(2), 133–154.

Masten, A. S., Best, K. M., & Garmezy, N. (1990). Resilience and development: Contributions from the study of children who overcome adversity. *Development and Psychopathology, 2,* 425–444.

McGrath, H., & Noble, T. (2010). Supporting positive pupil relationships: Research to practice. *Educational and Child Psychology, 27*(1), *British Psychology Society.*

Newman, T. (2004). What works in building resilience? Retrieved June 23, 2013, from http://www.barnardos.org.uk/what_works_in_building_resilience__-_summary_1_.pdf

Pepler, D., & Craig, W. (2000). Making a difference in bullying. Retrieved June 12, 2013, from http://www.melissainstitute.org/documents/MakingADifference.pdf

Reivich, K. J., Seligman, M. E., & McBride, S. (2011). Master resilience training in the U.S. Army. *American Psychology, 66,* 25–34.

Salmivalli, C. (2007). *From Peer Putdowns to Peer Support: The National Anti- bullying Program in Finland,* NCAB Conference Presentation, 2007, Melbourne, Australia. Retrieved April 10, 2013, from www.ncab.org.au/reading.html

Sawyer, M.G., Arney, F.M., Baghurst, P.A., Clark, J.J., Graetz, B.W., Kosky, R.J. et al. (2001 December). The mental health of young people in Australia: key findings from the child and adolescent component of the national survey of mental health and well- being. *Aust N Z J Psychiatry, 35*(6),806–14.

Sourander, A., Brunstein Klomek, A., Ikonen, M., Lindroos, J., Luntamo T., Koskelainen, M., Ristkari, T et al. (2010). Psychosocial risk factors associated with cyberbullying among adolescents: a population-based study. *Archives of General Psychiatry, 67,* 720–728.

Ungar, M. (2008). *CYM (The Child and Youth Resilience Measure),* International Resilience Project. Canada: Dalhousie University, Nova Scotia.

Vreeman, R. C., & Carroll, A. E. (2007). A systematic review of school-based interventions to prevent bullying. *Archives of Pediatric Adolescent Medicine, 161*(1), 78–88.

World Health Organisation (WHO). (2011). Retrieved July 6, 2013, from www.who.int/features/factfiles/mental_health/en/index.html

Wyn, J., Cuervo, H., Woodman, D., & Stokes, H. (2005). *Young people, wellbeing and communication technologies.* Melbourne: VicHealth.

Chapter 4
Educational Approaches

Abstract Bullying in schools has always existed and recently we have realised it is a symptom of a dysfunctional social system. Young people engage with online environments to the extent they blend with their offline worlds. A similar approach should be adopted when developing educational approaches. Cyberbullying is a behavioural issue, not a technological problem. Whole-school educational approaches which focus on behavioural change have been found to be the most successful. Effective policy is the backbone to good practice in schools, and internet safety should be no exception. The only way change can be brought about is through the systematic teaching of skills and strategies to help students when they encounter a cyberbullying situation. Young people need to be involved in the development of appropriate educational materials. Educating adults is also seen to be as important as educating young people about internet safety. Communication and relationships between school and home are important in dealing effectively with cyberbullying. Promoting socially acceptable behaviour is an effective strategy. Cyber-safety is essential for all young people and therefore needs to be embedded into the curriculum and teaching young people a range of social and emotional skills will assist them to navigate cyber-safety risks is considered to be an effective prevention strategy.

Keywords Whole-school · Cybersafety · Educational materials · Programs · Empowering young people · Cultural change · School climate · Parents · Social and emotional learning

4.1 Whole-School Approaches

The internet and other digital and information and communication technologies (ICT) are important tools, which provide new opportunities and challenges for everyone. ICT assists teachers and students to learn from each other and can stimulate discussion, promote creativity and an awareness of context to promote

S. Chadwick, *Impacts of Cyberbullying, Building Social and Emotional Resilience in Schools*, SpringerBriefs in Education, DOI: 10.1007/978-3-319-04031-8_4, © The Author(s) 2014

effective learning. Students with internet access are more confident and have been shown to produce better-researched and more effective projects.

A wider duty of care is a requirement to ensure children and young people are able to use the internet and related ICT appropriately and safely especially within the school context. A framework of internet safety policies, agreements or initiatives may ensure young people's use is safe and appropriate. Embedding safe internet practices into the culture of the school and the development and implementation of such strategies should involve all the stakeholders in a child's education (i.e. executive, teachers, parents and other students).

An effective approach requires clearly defined responsibilities, reporting lines and communication essential in the context of the time and other resource challenges staff have to manage. School staff with responsibility for pastoral care/student wellbeing, behaviour and IT systems, as well as the school council, parents and teacher unions/professional associations representing staff, will need to work together.

The development of high-quality learning environments which build a range of pro-social skills for children and young people is a key factor. Focusing on being responsible, critical thinking, reflective thinking, listening to others, solving problems in creative and non-violent ways, communicating clearly, participating in discussions, arguing thoughtfully and collaboratively working towards a common goal[1] are the foundation for engaging young people.

The first step in dealing with the complex issue of cyberbullying is to acknowledge it occurs by raising awareness. Schools need to develop a range of educational approaches and strategies to achieve shared understandings, informed planning and collaborative action among all groups within the school community to develop effective strategies to reduce the prevalence of cyberbullying.

Further to this, Rigby[2] investigated six intervention strategies to support schools in dealing with bullying behaviours.

- The traditional disciplinary approach;
- Strengthening the victim;
- Mediation;
- Restorative Practices;
- The Support Group Method; and
- The Method of Shared Concern.

He also suggests these approaches are not mutually exclusive. Whole-school approaches enable students to assist and support those who are being cyberbullied and develop skills for the bystanders to intervene. Improving classroom management and engaging students could also lead to a reduction in cyberbullying behaviours.

---

[1] Cohen (2006).

[2] Rigby (2010).

The Australian Covert Bullying Prevalence Study (ACBPS),[3] found the perceptions of the school's culture regarding cyberbullying was significant both for those who engage in cyberbullying behaviours and those who are cyberbullied.

Effective school leadership is key to the creation of a positive school culture. Organisational and leadership practices in schools can sustain and strengthen management practices, the level of supervision and enhance prevention strategies. They also provide a strong basis for effective whole-school approaches against offline and online bullying behaviours.

As a minimum to a whole-school approach, schools should develop an 'acceptable use policy/agreement' to protect the interests of both students and staff. This needs to be linked to other mandatory school policies such as child protection, home-school agreements, and student wellbeing or discipline (including an anti-bullying) policy. Internet safety policies should be regularly monitored and reviewed, and all staff should be aware of the appropriate strategies they should adopt if they encounter problems. Additionally, all school staff have a duty to ensure students using ICT, in any context, are reminded about appropriate behaviour on a regular basis. Effective policy is the backbone to good practice in schools, and internet safety should be no exception. Good policy is based on actual strategies for dealing with internet safety incidents should they occur. Key components of an effective 'acceptable use policy/agreement' include:

- clarity on rights and responsibilities of users, and penalties for breaches;
- signed by students and parents;
- information sessions on cyber-safety prior to policy/agreement being endorsed; and
- supported by policies which are understood by staff, students and parents.

Developing a whole-school approach to deal with cyberbullying commences with an audit of the strategies, initiatives, programs and practices already in place within the school community and the range of resources which may be available (Fig. 4.1).

Developing and implementing a policy involves key steps:

- articulate a clear procedure and code of conduct and ensure staff and parents are aware of how to deal with a breach of policy.
- consult with staff, parents and, where appropriate, students on the draft policies and codes of conduct. Revise as required from feedback.
- promote policies and codes of conduct, specifically the rules associated with each policy and the consequences of breaking any rules.
- policies and codes of conduct to be accessible to parents (i.e. for signature or sighting and provided in easy-to-read format or appropriate language).
- establish and promote a key cyber-safety person, or several people, as a first point of contact for students, staff and parents if a cyber-safety issue arises.

---

[3] Cross et al. (2009a, b).

Fig. 4.1 Whole-school audit

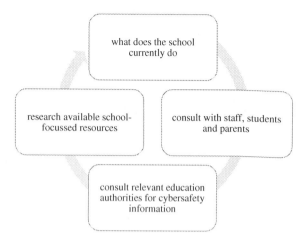

what does the school
currently do

research available school-
focussed resources

consult with staff, students
and parents

consult relevant education
authorities for cybersafety
information

- review policies and procedures annually as technologies and the use of them evolves rapidly.

Effectively addressing cyberbullying means making sure the whole-school community knows cyberbullying is not acceptable and is aware of how to identify and take action against cyberbullying. Schools can take pro-active measures to help prevent cyberbullying from occurring, and to reduce the impact of any incidents which may occur.

Rigby and Slee[4] have highlighted a number of issues concerning the nature of offline bullying in Australian schools for over a decade. Those findings are summarised below.

- The number of students who report being bullied at least weekly between 8–17 years of age is about 1 in 4. It is higher for boys.
- There are large differences between primary and secondary schools, with children in primary schools experiencing offline bullying much more frequently.
- 1 in 10 students has reported being an active 'bully'—many children admit to it and some boast of bullying others.
- In all age groups the extent of verbal bullying is similar for boys and girls.
- Girls are less likely to be physically bullied than boys.
- Physical bullying becomes less frequent with age compared with other forms of bullying.
- Verbal bullying becomes more frequent comparatively with age.
- Bullying decreases with age, reducing more quickly for girls than for boys.
- Boys bully far more often than girls do, but bully indirectly less often than girls.
- In primary schools, boys and girls are bullied more or less equally—in secondary schools boys are targeted more.

---

[4] Rigby and Slee (2001).

- There is no evidence there is a difference in the level of bullying between co-educational and single sex schools.
- Group bullying is more likely to be encountered by girls.
- 80 % of students act as bystanders, teachers are rarely present.
- 57 % of bullying behaviours stop when peers intervene.

In 2007 the *Kandersteg Declaration* Against Bullying in Children and Youth[5] was developed. It states some key considerations and actions.

Considerations

- many risk factors and protective factors associated with bullying are known and prevention programs are being implemented in several countries with promising results;
- mental, and physical health, social and academic consequences of bullying have an enormous impact on human and social capital; and
- bullying concerns and affects us all.

Actions

- start prevention efforts early and continue these through childhood and adolescence, targeting known and protective factors and promoting healthy relationships;
- educate and empower all adults involved with children and young people to promote healthy relationships and prevent bullying; and
- use policy and prevention programs, based on scientific research, which are appropriate for age, gender and culture and involve families, peers, schools and communities.

Bullying behaviours impact on the climate of a school whether students are directly or indirectly involved. Other students serve as reinforcers and models of behaviour, and consequently classrooms containing high numbers of students with poor academic skills or behaviour problems are likely to promote these behaviours in individual students.[6] Poorer classroom environments were associated with poorer levels of student aggression, peer relations and academic focus.

Students who are witnessing bullying behaviours occurring can often feel anger, guilt, fear, powerlessness and sadness toward the student being bullied.[7] At times they can also experience the same negative feelings as those being bullied. Bystanders report a similar, if not greater, psychological impact as they believe the same behaviours could happen to them in the future. Many students also feel guilty for not being able to intervene.

---

[5] Kandersteg (2007).

[6] Barth et al. (2004).

[7] Batsche and Porter (2006).

A culture within schools can also be created where bullying behaviours are accepted due to the feelings of powerlessness and isolation.[8] Research indicates some students believe bullying behaviours could not be prevented in their schools.

The only way change can be brought about is through the systematic teaching of skills and strategies to help students when they encounter a cyberbullying situation. Students need to be taught how to recognise cyberbullying when it occurs and how to deal appropriately with such incidents.[9] This may include direct intervention, reporting or a combination of both. Students need to be supported in their endeavours to bring cyberbullying into the offline world so they can be addressed in a positive manner.

There is evidence to support the notion intervention programs can be successful in reducing bullying behaviours in schools. Intervention programs which are implemented with younger primary school aged students are likely to have the greatest success. These interventions should also include a whole-school approach to raising awareness amongst staff and parents, the revision of existing policies and procedures and social skills development for students. Smith, Pepler and Rigby's review[10] on successful interventions indicate how well students relate to each other as being key to reducing bullying behaviours. There is strong evidence other students are an effective method for assisting those who are bystanders to improve relationships and they are accepted and valued for their contribution to empowering young people who are bystanders in any bullying incident and provides a program for effecting positive cultural change in school contexts.

Pressure to rapidly solve cyberbullying can lead school communities to react to incidents or seek out externally produced, one-off programs. These 'quick fix' solutions do little to address the broader social and historical perspectives as to why students engage in bullying behaviours both offline and online. A positive school culture is one which responds to all bullying behaviours by changing attitudes and beliefs and building upon existing strategies. These strategies are designed to further develop and enhance a positive school culture supporting responsible personal behaviour and effective teaching and learning. Coordinated whole-school community responses to cyberbullying prevention and management should be embedded into positive behavioural expectations and student wellbeing practices to ensure there are consistent messages.

4.1.1 Cybersafety

Online environments present new opportunities and new challenges for schools and parents. Even the words used to refer to this area can vary from cyber-safety, cyber-security, cyberbullying, cyber-citizenship, online safety or security, internet

---

[8] Salmivalli and Voeten (2004).

[9] Chadwick (2010).

[10] Smith, Pepler and Rigby (2004).

safety or security, or digital citizenship. However, cyber-safety is more commonly used and defined as the safe and responsible use of ICT. Cyber-safety education should begin in early childhood as this is an important time to develop skills and qualities such as respect, empathy, responsibility, sense of community and even leadership. In addition, children between the ages of 8–12 years are considered to be the most vulnerable online, so early education is paramount to minimise the negative impacts of cyberbullying and develop positive wellbeing.

Most adults would not consider it responsible to buy a young person a car and then allow them to drive without any learning or demonstrating a level of knowledge and skills to avoid the dangers on the road. We also probably wouldn't expect the police to be able to protect them while they are driving to prevent them from having an accident. However, this is what we do with technology for young people, we provide them mobile phones, access to the internet and a range of other electronic devices without teaching them about cyber-safety and then expect adult authorities to protect them from each other.

Cyber-safety practices should be developed from an early age and begin at home. Recently, in Australia, a nation-wide program developed by the Alannah and Madeline Foundation[11] will be trialed. Children between the ages of 8–12 years will sit for a 'digital licence' to prove they are safe online before parents allow them to log on. Parents will also have access to reports on how their child is progressing compared with those of a similar age. The aim of the program is to teach the skills of being safe online and developing skills in resilience and protective behaviours (Fig. 4.2).

The key elements to implementing cyber-safety approaches are:

- whole-school approach—assists in preventing and dealing with cyberbullying;
- access to professional development—for staff to continue to provide support;
- review and evaluate—technologies change rapidly and policies and practices need to be up-to-date;
- focus on behaviour—address the cause of the cyberbullying (i.e. power, intent, relationships) by educating everyone;
- do not restrict use—young people are less likely to report cyberbullying if they fear their access will be restricted or banned; and
- visible access—ensure staff can view the use of technology in open spaces.

Young people need to learn the skills in making developmentally appropriate and wise decisions about their engagement in the online world. Restricting use and banning technology is not the answer to dealing with cyberbullying as much of a young person's social world is linked to technology. Offline bullying behaviours flourish in secrecy due to the reluctance to report, cyberbullying will also increase if young people fear restriction of access could be the result from reporting. Young people need adults to support and guide them in the ethical and responsible use of

---

[11] AMF (2013).

Fig. 4.2 Cybersafety approach

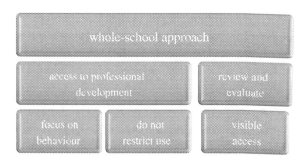

technology. The notion of 'do what is right, because it is right' is important to instil in young people.

Encouraging young people to tell someone what is happening is as essential as developing resilience and coping skills. Young people need to identify who can support them (i.e. Fig. 3.1 I have, I am, I can model) and have the confidence and skills to communicate their feelings. While school communities are instrumental in teaching young people about cyber-safety and online ethics, a great deal of the influence on young people is outside the school community. A whole-of-community issue is being discussed in regard to cyber-safety education as schools are complex and have increasing demands on time (i.e. crowded curriculum, assessments) that to address the issue of cyberbullying and cyber-safety in schools alone would be missing the opportunity to capitalise on the help-seeking capacity of young people. In addition, cyber-safety issues occur across a range of locations therefore a whole-community solution needs to be adopted in order to address the multiple modes in which young people access the online environment. Young people are part of the problem, they should also be part of the solution.

4.1.2 Appropriate Educational Materials

Determining the most appropriate resources for use in schools and to teach young people about cyber-safety is challenging. Internet searches alone for cyber-safety resources can result in over 2 million 'hits' and it is overwhelming to know where to start. A central, government based and funded repository of resources for teachers, young people and parents to access have been suggested in Australia which has a national focus. However, the coordination and logistics of such a proposal add further challenges.

Young people need to be involved in the development of appropriate educational materials or, at the very least, be consulted about what should and should not be included. After all, they are the experts in the online world. The materials developed should also be accessed through the mediums by which young people use (i.e. social media, email etc.). Promoting material on government websites seems to have limited impact on young people, they are not the type of websites they would naturally access for information. Sites developed specifically for young people which have the 'look' and 'feel' to engage with this group are more likely to be successful. In recent times there has been the development of a range of smart phones applications which young people can access for information and education. Pop-ups on webpages are also effective in reinforcing cyber-safety messages, if these are not disabled or subjected to filters.

Educating adults is also seen to be as important as educating young people about internet safety and use. Encouraging social networking sites to have 'user-friendly' privacy setting functions and information has also been suggested. Positive messages which promote positive behaviours are needed within any strategy aimed at either reducing cyberbullying or increasing cyber-safety. Strategies also need to be 'attractive' to young people and use their 'language'. Many young people state the material available online for cyber-safety is aimed at adults and/or professionals. The majority of what young people learn is from their peers, not necessarily from adults. Educational material needs to reflect this.

Valuing existing knowledge of young people and building on this with appropriate and creative resources is key. Education which encourages young people to reflect on the real-life consequences caused by cyberbullying, sexting, a negative digital reputation etc. are increasingly successful and more importantly what young people want. The themes of personal and peer safety and responsibility may be crucial to maintaining positive online behaviour and digital reputation into adulthood. In general, young people comment they do know how to be safe online, as they are 'lectured' on what to post and what not to post, what they want more of, is to be informed about the consequences (i.e. legal consequences) of online behaviour. These are the messages young people believe will 'get through to them' especially if delivered by someone who 'has gone through it.'

A recent Australian Government initiative, available on all computers in all schools, is the Cyber-safety Help Button. It is designed to keep children and families safe online. It is an online resource hub providing instant 24 h access to cyber-safety help and information. The button has three features where children and young people can talk, report or learn about cyber-safety issues (Fig. 4.3).

Young people need to be responsible for their own experiences online and education, knowledge and skills will assist them in making better decisions. Focusing on the technology itself will not necessarily mean young people are cyber safe, a focus on the motivations behind decisions made will create greater cyber-safety. Cyberbullying is a behavioural issue, not a technological problem. Enhanced privacy provisions, more research and educating parents/teachers and others who interact with young people are essential. There are a vast array of stakeholders' involved in promoting cyber-safety to young people ranging from governments, industry, organisations, schools and parents. However, these stakeholders need to work together, and not in isolation, to develop coordinated and planned approaches to dealing with cybersafety.

Fig. 4.3 Cybersafety help
button (DBCDE 2010)

4.1.3 Peer Education and Empowering Young People

Peer-driven student leadership based programs are an effective means to encourage
positive relationships and open discussions about what occurs online and even
offline. Young people want to be involved in the educative process. Mentor groups
or youth advisory groups, for example, comprised of young people are more likely
to engage and connect with other young people. Assigning trained cyber-safety
student leaders can assist the wider school community to gain increased awareness
of the challenges in the online environment and changes to technology. Presentations developed and facilitated by young people leave a lasting impression and
the messages remain for longer than when adults present to young people.
Involving young people in the creative development of a range of mediums
(i.e. artwork, posters, infographics, vox pops etc.) will be more effective and
provide the opportunity for them to have ownership of the messages and education.
Young people have the capacity to positively influence social norms and discourage
cyberbullying and programs which develop student leadership and pro-social peer
structures are effective.

The development of positive peer relationships to promote pro-social behaviour
includes restorative practices, peer support structures such as peer counselling,
peer mediation, peer mentoring/buddy systems and peer tutoring.[12] Promoting
socially acceptance behaviour is an effective strategy. The development of social

---

[12] Stanley and McGrath (2006).

skills and cross-age interactions within schools assists young people to feel less isolated if cyberbullying occurs as evidence demonstrates having even one good friend can protect against the harmful consequences. Young people should be encouraged to have a wide variety of friends, both formal and informal, from a range of places, not just at school.

In a study conducted by Palladino[13] it was found peer educators were able to be agents of change in their classes rather than only benefiting from the intervention program. The same study found the most important program elements associated with a decrease in victimisation were also videos and cooperative group work and used in a framework of a peer-led model. If they are supported in their capacity to promote initiatives and active participation of other students, the process of change can involve the entire class and thereby the school community over time.

Initiatives need to empower young people to promote and monitor their own safety. Most young people obtain information from each other no matter what the subject. Young people may discuss with each other what are safe practices or highlight sites or posts which they sense are not ok though they do not necessarily inform their parents or teachers. There needs to be ways to encourage young people to work together collaboratively to make a stand and to share their experiences and perspectives. Young people should be encouraged to respond and can use a suggested 3 step model: stop, block, tell.[14]

- Stop the correspondence;
- Block the user; and
- Tell an adult.

Restorative justice programs are based on shared ownership to resolve issues of cyberbullying which may arise within schools. They take the form of conferences involving teachers, parents, students, community members and police. This is an educative process and are used widely in schools to empower young people to discuss the issue and find a range of solutions. The aim is to develop an understanding amongst students of the social and emotional impact of their behaviour—to focus on restoring an appropriate relationship.

Research has shown strengths-based programs are more effective and the results are more sustainable. Focusing on what is working well in supporting young people deal with all forms of bullying—offline and online. Young people have existing skills, knowledge and competencies and are capable of problem solving and learning new skills. Young people are part of the process in strengths-based programs. Promoting and developing the language and concepts of strengths-based approaches is also effective (i.e. care, positive feelings, empathy, mutual responsibility).

Encouraging young people to engage with other support services and agencies can be important in reducing the negative impacts of cyberbullying on their

---

[13] Palladino et al. (2012).

[14] STOP Cyberbullying n.d. (2013).

wellbeing. Mental health professionals can provide advice and support beyond the expertise of most teachers and parents.

4.1.4 Cultural Change

Cyberbullying is most often seen as occurring in a social context. The school culture, the actions and interactions of students and teachers and even the characteristics of the school's physical environment have some influence. A school's culture manifests itself in many different ways both direct and indirect. Core values embedded within a school such as respect, compassion and acceptance of differences are useful in maintaining a positive culture. When teachers are positive role models for inclusive behaviours then students are more likely to act in these ways too. However, when teachers use behaviour management strategies which are based on dominance and submission, they model this type of behaviour for students. Students who are already prone to engaging in bullying behaviours, offline or online, may then feel justified in bullying others and also believe these behaviours are acceptable.

Young people's perception of the culture of their school environment is influenced by their own behaviour or involvement in either offline or online bullying. Young people who are involved in bullying feel less safe and less connected to the school. They are also at a greater risk of experiencing social and emotional problems. Student disruption and poor classroom management are linked to their perception of the culture of the school. Reactive and punitive strategies tend to send negative messages to young people and the wider community. There is a point in schools where the level of disruption begins to negatively influence perceptions of the culture. However, the elimination of offline and online bullying in schools is not realistic so it would be useful to determine the point where they collectively become problematic within the school and target programs and interventions accordingly. Positive changes to culture are affected when there is a focus on creating an environment which enhances positive relationships across the school community. A positive 'tipping point' highlighting how many students seek help, intervene and are willing to do so on behalf of others to affect the culture and reduce cyberbullying would be useful data for schools.

School culture is difficult to define however, understanding it is critical to ensure positive changes are initiated to deal with cyberbullying. The National Safe Schools Framework (NSSF)[15] developed in Australia describes a safe and supportive school in the following way: In a safe and supportive school, the risk from all types of harm is minimised, diversity is valued and all members of the school community feel respected and included and can be confident that they will receive support in the face of any threats to their safety or wellbeing.

---

[15] NSSF (2011).

A whole-school approach to creating safe and supportive learning and teaching communities acknowledges the strong interconnections between student wellbeing and learning and cultural change. A whole-school approach is inclusive of staff, students and parents. Offline and online bullying behaviours are less likely to occur in caring, respectful and supportive school communities.

The enhancement of a safe and supportive school environment is a broad concept and its effective implementation will involve a range of integrated and collaborative strategies. A whole-school approach ensures students learn appropriate behaviours and skills through the formal and informal curriculum, classroom practices and other students. These are further supported by an individual schools' anti-bullying policy, procedures for reporting and current practices within their student wellbeing policies. Organisational and leadership practices in schools can sustain and strengthen management practices, the level of supervision and enhance prevention strategies.

Culture influences all aspects of schools and is constantly constructed through interactions with others and a common language. In effect, culture guides the behaviour which is shared amongst teachers, students and parents and is unique to each school community. Culture is also highly resilient and resistant to change. Teachers and the leadership within the school are the cornerstone to cultural change. Hargreaves[16] noted three characteristics of teachers which effect cultural change:

- years of teaching;
- sense of efficacy; and
- verbal ability.

The longer a teacher is in the same school the less likely they would adopt change and new programs or practices. The individual teachers' belief they can influence the most unmotivated student has a positive impact on change and the verbal ability of the individual teacher also is key. Power relationships in schools are also a barrier to cultural change.

Schools where there is a high degree of cooperation, collaboration, responsibility and accountability and where young people are involved and included in the decision making processes are the most effective in achieving positive culture. Skilling young people in important aspects such as critical thinking, problem solving and decision making are vital. Empowering all staff to respond effectively to classrooms disruptions, playground incidents and conflict without the need to constantly refer upwards, is key to minimising cyberbullying. Staff need to be aware they are all responsible for addressing offline and online bullying in the school even if they have no direct teaching or wellbeing responsibility for specific students. Cyberbullying needs to be viewed through a relational lens and the factors contributing to the relationship breakdown explored. For example, an issue on the playground may be viewed as non-compliance whereas it may be due to lack of

---

[16] Hargreaves (1997).

social skills or boredom. Key questions for staff to consider when discussing changes to be implemented if there are a range of playground incidents are:

Environment

Are there suitable active areas?
Is there a designated area for ball games?
Is there a designated quiet area for students?
Is the environment pleasant and feel relaxed? Does it encourage students to want to be there?

Supervision

Is the current supervision adequate?
Are we focusing supervision at potential risk areas? e.g. toilets
How do we give extra support if we have a playground incident?
What strategies are in place for managing playground behaviour?
How can student leaders' assist?

Activities

What equipment and activities are available for students?
Do we need lunch time clubs?
What role can the senior students or school leaders play in providing lunchtime activities?
Do we need to teach students appropriate playground games?

Extending these elements to cyberbullying can be addressed by considering the potential for promoting positive uses of technology and making new technology available to young people for both educational and social functions. Schools could utilise online or web-based reporting mechanisms as this appears to encourage more students to report both offline and online bullying.

The first step in dealing with the complex issue of cyberbullying is to acknowledge it occurs by raising awareness. The following elements can assist in understanding cyberbullying and create an environment for cultural change:

- consistent understandings;
- include parents;
- restorative practices;
- focus on behaviour and positive language;
- gather information;
- model pro-social behaviours; and
- use the method of shared concern.

Schools need to develop strategies to achieve shared understandings, informed planning and collaborative action among all groups within the school community to develop effective cyberbullying strategies. There also needs to be consistency amongst staff in dealing with cyberbullying by demonstrating a link between the school's policy and procedures and the actual programs and practices. This can be

Table 4.1 Dimensions of school climate[a]

1. Safety	• Rules and norms
	• Physical safety
	• Social and emotional security
2. Teaching and learning	• Support for learning
	• Social and civic learning
3. Interpersonal relationships	• Respect for diversity
	• Social support—adults
	• Social support—students
4. Institutional environment	• School connectedness and engagement
	• Physical surroundings

[a] Cohen et al. (2009)

achieved by modelling pro-social values in teaching and classroom organisation and interactions.

Educational approaches and programs which address cyberbullying may have more effect in changing attitudes than reducing the actual bullying behaviours. This fact should not be discounted, as changing attitudes is essential in changing school culture and student behaviour. School culture has a significant impact on student wellbeing, social and emotional resilience and academic success as well as a range of staff outcomes however, there are few programs which have been developed for school culture.

Connectedness and social and emotional resilience are important aspects in creating and maintaining a positive school culture. Schools which encourage student connectedness to teachers through extra-curricular activities are supportive. An important strategy for cyberbullying is creating opportunities for promoting bystander intervention[17] by encouraging a supportive peer culture in schools (Table 4.1).

4.1.5 Parents

The time to reach parents is when children are between 1–5 years old and it is important they engage positively in the online world. Parents' involvement in the safe use of technology begins from the child's first use. Recreational use of the internet begins in the home and cyber-safety messages need to be taught just as we teach our children how to cross the road safely. Parenting children in the online world should be no different than the offline world. Children need to be set appropriate boundaries and limits. Parents have a vital role in preventing and responding to cyberbullying, monitoring and teaching safe internet use and communicating with their children.

---

[17] Salmivalli (2010).

Monitoring internet usage is proven to be a successful strategy for parents to adopt and it should start at a young age. Parents are the primary role models for children and if they are engaging with their children by monitoring the sites visited and what is on the screen, children will learn responsible digital citizenship. Excessive monitoring by parents can also be detrimental to young people by limiting their ability to learn experientially and to become independent. Just as we teach children how to cross the road safely, at some point we need to let go of their hand. However, finding the balance between monitoring and fostering independence is a challenge for many parents.

Factors evident which make it challenging for parents to monitor their children's internet usage include:[18]

- screen not being visible to view at all times, especially with wireless and mobile phone connections;
- access which is occurring within school time;
- amounts of time young people spend online;
- resistance to time limits;
- preventing exposure to inappropriate content;
- children's control of passwords, web browser history, phone locks etc.; and
- keeping pace with changes in technology especially social networking and virtual sites.

The perception young people have about their parents' knowledge with technology influences the level of acceptance and the value they place on the advice. Adults use technology for business or practical purposes though an increasing number of them are using it to monitor their children's usage. The fact many parents are actually unaware of the capabilities of technology has seen the need for young people to assist their parents with cyber-safety (Table 4.2).

However, young people are the experts with technology and often adopt a 'teaching' role for their parents who want to develop their own skills and digital literacy. Parents have limited understanding of the reasons why young people engage with technology to the extent they do. In addition, this generation of parents may have insufficiently developed digital literacy as they are learning through their children rather than having grown up with technology. Encouraging intergenerational conversations about technology use is paramount in an attempt to bridge the 'digital divide'. Being with children whist they are using technology and starting a conversation with them about how to use it assists with developing practical strategies to support online safety.

Parents may lack the skills and knowledge to learn about online safety or where to access reliable information. Some are ill equipped to support their children with the complex issue of cyber-safety, have limited technical skills and are less familiar with the various platforms and sites young people use. Young people need to have adults (i.e. parents or teachers) who are confident and knowledgeable in the

---

[18] ACMA (2007).

Table 4.2 Social media, young people and parents[a]

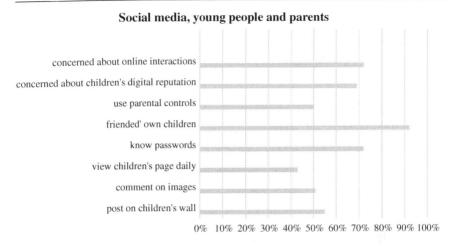

Social media, young people and parents

concerned about online interactions

concerned about children's digital reputation

use parental controls

friended' own children

know passwords

view children's page daily

comment on images

post on children's wall

0% 10% 20% 30% 40% 50% 60% 70% 80% 90% 100%

[a] Pew Research Centre (2012)

online world to support them to engage in safe, smart, respectful and responsible ways.

Addressing cyberbullying when it occurs can be most effective when the young person is willing to tell a parent and the parent has the capacity to respond appropriately. Parents need strategies to respond positively to cyberbullying other than restricting or banning the use of technology. As discussed, young people are less likely to report cyberbullying to their parents if they believe their access will be denied.

Identifying when a child has been cyberbullied if they are reluctant to tell parents are similar to the indicators of offline bullying behaviours (i.e. mood changes, difficulty sleeping, and loss of interest in activities). Parents are in the best position to notice any changes in their child's demeanour or actions, after all, parents should know their children well enough to see a change. Reporting incidents to the school as soon as possible is also critical as most cyberbullying occurs outside of school.

Key points for parents in preventing cyberbullying:

- increase knowledge and become more adept with technology;
- understand why technology is important to children;
- discuss online engagement and learn about what children are accessing;
- develop on online plan for all family members;
- communicate about monitoring; and
- access cyber-safety resources.

A strengths-based emphasis for parents and families is also critical. Concentrating on what parents are doing right, rather than focusing on what they are doing wrong. Parents should also be encouraged to look for the strengths their children are demonstrating through their actions. Building on this leads to a sense of hope and optimism for the future and can make a difference in enhancing positive behaviours and reducing both offline and online bullying behaviours.

4.1.6 Curriculum and Programs

The primary aim of education is for young people to be responsible citizens in current and future contexts. Cyber-safety is essential for all young people and therefore needs to be embedded into the curriculum. Teachers need to manage offline and online learning environments within a social construct where relationships for many young people are fluid and dynamic. Supporting students to navigate their social and emotional needs when they are engaging in online environments and achieve academic outcomes is complex. Investigating whether cyber-safety education should also be included in pre-service teaching programs may be effective.

Digital citizenship requires young people to know their rights and also their responsibilities online. Teaching sound digital and media literacy in schools, libraries, youth clubs and at parent evenings is a starting point. Young people and adults need to develop an understanding about how the range of digital devices work and how to manipulate them, while gaining greater knowledge, wisdom and discernment about the content they provide.

The Melbourne Declaration on Educational Goals for Young Australians[19] made important points about ICT in curriculum:

- young people need to be highly skilled in its use;
- development of skills in areas such as social interaction, cross-disciplinary thinking and the use of digital media in twenty-first century occupations;
- essential literacy and numeracy skills and are creative and productive users of technology; and
- practical knowledge and skills development.

Communication and relationships between school and home are important in dealing effectively with cyberbullying. Raising awareness amongst parents enhances partnerships between home and school. The development of policy, processes and procedures which are collaborative are also successful. However, a range of studies indicated whilst cyberbullying and cyber-safety programs increase awareness, there is limited evidence to demonstrate changes in behaviour. This

---

[19] MCEETYA (2008).

may be due to the fact this is relatively new area of study and behavioural change takes a while to be affected.

Generally, successful programs should include:

- component for all students—universal intervention;
- component for students who engage in bullying behaviours and those who are bullied—indicated interventions; and
- component for bystanders—reduces motivation for those who engage in bullying behaviours.

Many schools however will need to individualise programs by adapting or combining aspects of existing published programs or by adding complimentary components such as values education or social skills etc. Modifications may also need to be made to existing programs to cater for the different ways both females and males use technology and how they engage in the online environment. Females and males are also motivated to participate in offline and online bullying behaviours differently.

Programs which offer a range of developmentally and age-appropriate activities embedded into the curriculum will have a greater impact than a one-off program. Topic areas such as:

- internet safety;
- privacy and security;
- relationships and communication;
- cyberbullying;
- digital footprint and reputation;
- self-image and identity;
- digital literacy; and
- social and emotional resilience

could be useful to develop.

In Australia two examples of effective cyber-safety programs are eSmart and Cybersmart.

eSmart[20]—The Alannah and Madeline Foundation—eSmart is an easy-to-use, evidence-based and tested system, providing a framework approach to help improve cyber-safety and wellbeing in Australian schools. Launched in 2011 there are now more than 1,500 schools participating. eSmart Schools is making a real difference in schools across all sectors and year levels, equipping them with the resources and knowledge to effectively create a school culture which embraces the positives of the online world for young people.

Being eSmart means knowing how to guard against the security and privacy risks online, download and upload content in a legal and ethical way, to research and reference information, as well as manage reputation and relationships in cyberspace. Using a behaviour-change approach, eSmart Schools aims to create a

---

[20] AMF (2013).

community of students, teachers and parents who are smart, safe and responsible with technology. Once registered with eSmart Schools, schools are supported to:

- create their own best—practice policies, practices and procedures;
- gain access to the best evidence—informed resources and information; and
- record, track and report on their progress.[21]

There are six domains which emphasise an integrated and holistic approach and encourage the creation of a common language. Schools who develop initiatives and programs across all domains will, overtime, achieve sustained cultural change. The six domains are:

1. effective school organisation;
2. school plans, policies and procedures;
3. respectful and caring school community;
4. effective teacher practices;
5. a eSmart curriculum; and
6. partnerships with parents and local communities.

The key characteristics of eSmart are evidence-informed practices, positive approaches to technology; whole-school approaches to change and data driven and sustainable. These are underpinned by the values of responsibility, resourcefulness, relationships and respect.

Cybersmart[22]—The Australian Communications and Media Authority (ACMA)—Cybersmart is a national cyber-safety and cybersecurity education program managed by ACMA, as part of the Australian Government's commitment to cyber-safety. The program is specifically designed to meet the needs of its target audiences of children, young people, parents, teachers and library staff.

Cybersmart resources include a range of presentations and workshops for teachers, students and staff such as:

- internet safety awareness presentations;
- workshops;
- professional development programs; and
- pre-service teacher programs.

Cybersmart is designed to support and encourage participation in the digital economy by providing information and education which empowers children to be safe online. The principles of Cybersmart as outlined by AMCA are:

- It aims to develop 'digital citizens' who are able to derive the benefits of online participation while taking responsibility for self-protection by understanding the potential consequences of online behaviour. Digital citizenship goes beyond safety and risk, and encompasses the notion of positive engagement in the online environment.

---

[21] AMF (2013).

[22] ACMA (2013a, b).

- With a focus on digital engagement, the program is not designed to tackle issues for which a specialist response is needed, and will defer to the expertise of others. Such issues may include cyber-crime (requiring an enforcement response) or self-harming behaviours (requiring a mental health response).
- Cybersmart programs are research based. ACMA undertake regular research into the cyber-safety information needs of young people, their parents and their teachers. AMCA also pay attention to best practice research conducted nationally and internationally.
- All Cybersmart content and resources are created based on the same underlying principles: these materials are of a high standard, consistent, audience-appropriate and well prepared. Materials are assessed by their audiences on how suitable, effective, and engaging they are, and how easy they are to use. All materials bearing the Cybersmart brand are high quality and carefully reviewed prior to publishing.
- As a program funded by the Australian Government, Cybersmart is required to meet high standards of transparency, probity and audit. Program effectiveness is assessed through a continuing and formal evaluation program.
- Cybersmart looks actively to draw on the experience and skills of other internationally leading providers of cyber-safety education (for example NetSafe in New Zealand and Childnet International in the UK). Cybersmart will adapt and re-use materials and resources developed by such providers under appropriate agreements with the relevant providers where the materials are of high standard and directly meet the identified needs of the Cybersmart target audience.
- The ACMA will cooperate and collaborate with other organisations in Australia and overseas whose aims and approach are consistent with those of the Cybersmart program principles. In considering any such associations the ACMA will have regard to consistency of aims, approach and standards with the Cybersmart program and with the ACMA's probity and transparency obligations as a Government agency.[23]

Smart Online Safe Offline (SOSO) is an Australian initiative aimed at young people and developed in partnership with the National Association for the Prevention of Child Abuse and Neglect (NAPCAN). Cyber safety continues to be a key concern for Australian parents. SOSO brings together community, government and the digital media industry as partners to keep young internet users safe online.

By targeting children and young people directly—in their language and within their social networking environments—SOSO helps children and young people understand dangers which exist online and educates them about how to manage their personal safety both online and offline. SOSO is the only Australian initiative operating within the online space and social networking sites which raises awareness.

---

[23] ACMA (2013).

SOSO's first campaign was targeted to educate about the dangers of online predation. Reaching over 80 % of its target market, an independent evaluation found the campaign to have achieved statistically significant shifts in awareness, attitude and intended behaviour.

SOSO's second campaign targeted online bullying. This campaign seems to be making an impact with young people, according to their recent external evaluation of their anti-cyber bullying campaign. Their "Cyber Bullying—Bystander Behaviour" uses a YouTube video and educational game called "Web Warriors".[24]

Teaching young people a range of social and emotional skills will assist them to navigate cyber-safety risks and is considered to be an effective prevention strategy. Key skills important are:

- pro-social values—compassion, respect, acceptance;
- emotional skills—empathy, self-respect, impulse control;
- social skills—cooperation, managing conflict, relationships; and
- high-order thinking skills—critical analysis, problem solving.

Social skills are related to all aspects of behaviour in schools (i.e. classrooms, playground) and the learning programs need to be experiential. Social skills cannot be taught in isolation and need to be embedded into curriculum either as classroom-based programs or small group or individualised programs. The greatest success is where there is a structured program and key skills are explicitly taught. Students need to be taught why the skill is useful, followed by structured opportunities to practise the skill, feedback on use of the skill and opportunities to practice in real-world contexts. Students may be less likely to be the targets of cyberbullying if they learn:

- emotional skills—self-respect, resilience and managing negative emotions such as sadness, loneliness and anxiety; and
- social skills—assertiveness, conflict management, conversing and playing games and making and keeping friends.[25]

Social and Emotional Learning (SEL) programs provide students with basic social skills such as making sound decisions and refusal skills which enable them to avoid engaging in high-risk behaviours such as cyberbullying. Teachers and schools can improve social skills by creating learning contexts where skills are positively reinforced and frequently practised.

Schools have incorporated a range of cross-curriculum programs and initiatives to promote wellbeing and resilience in their students in the offline world. These programs could be expanded to promote cybersafety.

---

[24] SOSO (2013).
[25] Life Education (2012).

References

Alannah and Madeline Foundation. (2013). Retrieved July 9, 2013, from http://www.heraldsun. com.au/technology/news/cyber-licence-trial-for-children-to-make-sure-they-are-safe-online/ story-fni0bzod-1226673379998.

Australian Government, Department of Broadband, Communication and the Digital Economy. (2010). Retrieved July 13, 2013, from http://www.dbcde.gov.au/online_safety_and_security/ cybersafetyhelpbutton_download.

Australian Communications and Media Authority. (2007). *Media and communications in Australian families 2007: Report of the Media and Society Research Project.* Retrieved July 14, 2013, from www.acma.gov.au/scripts/nc.dll?WB/STANDARD/1001/pc=PC_310893.

Barth, J. M., Dunlap, S. T., Dane, H., Lochman, J. E., & Wells, K. C. (2004). Classroom environment influences of aggression, peer relations and academic focus. *Journal of School Psychology, 42*(2), 115–133.

Batsche, G. M., & Porter, J. (2006). Bullying In G. G. Bear & K. M. Minke (Eds.) *Children's Needs III: Development, Prevention and Intervention,* (pp. 135–14). Bethesda: National Association of School Psychologists.

Chadwick, S. (2010). *They Can't Hurt Me: A peer-led approach to bullying.* USA: VDM Publishing.

Cohen, J. (2006). Social, emotional, ethical and academic education: Creating a climate for learning, participation in democracy and wellbeing. *Harvard Education Review, 76*(2), 201–237.

Cohen, J., Pickeral, T., & McCloskey, M. (2009). The Challenge of Assessing School Climate. *Educational Leadership, Dec 2008/January 2009/January 2009, 66*(4), 28–32.

Cross, D., Shaw, T., Hearn, L., Epstein, M., Monks, H., Lester, L., et al. (2009a). *Australian Covert Bullying Prevalence Study (ACBPS),* Child Health Promotion Research Centre, Perth: Edith Cowan University. Retrieved May 4, 2013, from www.deewr.gov.au/Schooling/ NationalSafeSchools/Pages/research.aspx.

Cross, D., Shaw, T., Epstein, M., Monks, H., Lester, L., & Thomas, L. (2009b). *Australian Covert Bullying Prevalence Study (ACBPS),* Child Health Promotion Centre, Australia, Perth: Edith Cowan University. Retrieved July 9, 2013, from www.deewr.gov.au/schooling/ nationalsafeschools/pages/research.aspx.

Hargreaves, A. (1997). Introduction. In A Hargreaves (Ed.), *Rethinking educational change with heart and mind: 1997 ASCD yearbook* (pp. 815). Alexandria. Virginia: Association for Supervision and Curriculum Development.

Kandersteg Declaration. (2007). *Against Bullying and Youth.* Retrieved July 9, 2013, from www.kanderstegdeclaration.com/storage/English%20KD.pdf.

Kandersteg Declaration. (2007). *Against Bullying and Youth.* Retrieved July 9, 2013, from www.kanderstegdeclaration.com/storage/English%20KD.pdf.

Life Education Australia, prepared by McGrath, H. (2012). Students, cybersafety, relationships and Life Education: A literature review.

National Safe Schools Framework. (2011). *Australian Government Department of Education, Employment and Workplace Relations.* Canberra. Retrieved July 21, 2013, from http:// foi.deewr.gov.au/system/files/doc/other/national_safe_schools_framework.pdf.

Palladino, B. E., Nonentini, A., & Menesini, E. (2012). Online and offline peer led models against bullying and cyberbullying. *Psicothema, 24*(4), 634–639.

Pew Research Centre. (2012). USA. Retrieved July 14, 2013, from http://www.factbrowser.com/ tags/parents/.

Rigby, K. (2010). *Bullying intervention in schools. six basic approaches.* Victoria: ACER Press.

Rigby, K., & Slee, P. (2001). Bullying among Australian school children: Reported behaviours and attitudes to victims. *Journal of Social Psychology, 131,* 15–627.

Salmivalli, C. (2010). Bullying and the peer group: A review. *Aggression and Violent Behaviour, 15*(2), 112–120.

Salmivalli, C., & Voeten, M. (2004). Connections between attitudes, group norms and behaviours in bullying situations. *International Journal of Behavioural Development, 28*(3), 246–258.

Smart Online Safe Offline. (2013) Retrieved November 3, 2013, http://www.sos.org.au.

Smith, P. K., Pepler, D., & Rigby, K. (2004). *Bullying in Schools: How successful can interventions be?* Cambridge: Cambridge University Press.

Stanley, M., & McGrath, H. (2006). Buddy systems: Peer support in action. In H. L McGrath & T. Noble, *Bullying solutions: Evidence-based approaches.* Sydney: Pearson Education.

STOP cyberbullying (n.d.). *Stop, block and tell.* Retrieved July 14, 2013, from www.stopcyberbullying.org/taake_action/stop_block_and_tell.html.

The Alannah and Madeline Foundation. (2013a). Australia. Retrieved July 14, 2013, from http://www.esmart.org.au/Pages/default.aspx.

The Alannah and Madeline Foundation. (2013b). Australia. Retrieved November 3, 2013, from http://www.amf.org.au/Assets/Files/FactSheet_eSmart_new_June2013.pdf.

The Australian Communications and Media Authority .(2013a). Retrieved July 14, 2013, from http://www.cybersmart.gov.au/.

The Australian Communications and Media Authority. (2013b). Retrieved November 3, 2013, from http://www.cybersmart.gov.au/About%20Cybersmart/What%20is%20Cybersmart/Program%20principles.aspx.

The Ministerial Council for Employment, Education, Training and Youth Affairs (2008). Australia Retrieved July 14, 2013, from http://www.mceecdya.edu.au/verve/_resources/national_declaration_on_the_educational_goals_for_young_australians.pdf.

Chapter 5
Final Word

Abstract Promising interventions are those which take a whole-school approach. Dealing with the impacts of cyberbullying needs to take a socio-ecological perspective which includes an effective whole-school approach. Many countries have developed and are implementing a range of initiatives to deal with cyberbullying. The need for international collaborations in dealing with cyberbullying and promoting best-practice programs and strategies is important. Excessive regulation of young people and the use of technology does not provide for the learning of the skills they need to function in the 'real-world' post school. Regulating technology or taking legal action will not change behaviours. Schools have a well-established duty of care to their students and staff. This extends beyond reasonable precautions against physical injury and into psychological injury. Professional Development needs to address the attitudes and perceptions towards both offline and online bullying as well as the skills required to use the technology in effective teaching and learning programs. Cyberbullying directed towards teachers is increasing due to the anonymity of some online sites. Individual staff members or even the school itself can be the target of inappropriate content. When developing policies and procedures in schools, cyberbullying of staff should also be recognised.

Keywords International initiatives · Professional development · Teachers · Cyberbullying of staff · Law

5.1 International Initiatives

Teaching young people about positive relationships, empathy, conflict resolution skills such as anger management, problem solving, decision making and the importance of bystander intervention in schools is critical to dealing with the impacts of cyberbullying.

Promising interventions are those which take a whole-school approach aimed at:

S. Chadwick, *Impacts of Cyberbullying, Building Social and Emotional*   81
Resilience in Schools, SpringerBriefs in Education,
DOI: 10.1007/978-3-319-04031-8_5, © The Author(s) 2014

- enhancing a positive school climate and ethos which promotes pro-social behaviours;
- providing pre-service and in-service training of all school staff to assist them to recognise and respond appropriately to signs of cyberbullying;
- creating physical environments which limit the invisibility of cyberbullying;
- increasing the awareness among young people of how group mechanisms work and strengthening their skills in conflict resolution; and
- developing anonymous, peer-led support structures for students to access when they feel uncomfortable.[1]

Many countries have developed and are implementing a range of initiatives to deal with cyberbullying.

5.1.1 United Kingdom

In 2001 the Task Force on Child Protection on the Internet was established. It is a collaboration of representatives predominantly from the internet industry, children's charities, government departments and the police. In 2008 it published its 'Good Practice Guidance for the Providers of Social Networking and Other User Interactive Services'[2] providing:

- industry and others with safety advice;
- tips for children and young people; and
- guidance for parents/carers to ensure the safety of their children.

Documents similar to this have also been developed and promoted to industry groups such as the British code of practice for the self-regulation of new forms of content on mobile phones and the European Commission including Safer Social Networking Principles for the EU20 and the European Framework on Safer Mobile Use by Younger Teenagers and Children.[3]

The Child Exploitation and Online Protection Centre is a national law enforcement agency and operates the *ThinkUKnow*[4] website in Britain. This provides parents with a range of resources, information and webcasts which can assist them in protecting their children online. *ThinkUKnow* is also partnered by the Australian Federal Police and the site is now available in Australia.

UK Council for Child Internet Safety was established in 2008 and brings 140 organisations and individuals together to assist young people in being safe online. It's comprised of companies, government departments and agencies, law

---

[1] Cross et al. (2009).

[2] UK Council for Child Internet Safety (2010).

[3] Childnet International (2013).

[4] ThinkUKnow (2013).

enforcement, charities, parent groups and academic experts. A public awareness campaign named **'Click Clever Click Safe'**[5] promotes internet safety and has been found to raise awareness of the issue surrounding young people's online use.

The Office for Standards in Education, Children's Services and Skills has researched a range of initiatives and found the most effective schools in dealing with cyberbullying are those with a multi-faceted whole-school approach. A whole-school approach which includes and involves students, parents and teachers. The use of media campaigns to raise awareness and the development of mandated policies and procedures are considered key to the success of effective programs.

Childnet International is a British-based charity focused on education, awareness and policy. It has developed the ***Know IT All***[6] resources on cyberbullying designed for young people and parents to manage the risks they may encounter online.

5.1.2   United States

Online Safety and Technology Working Group was established in 2008 as part of the United States National Telecommunications and Information Administration. Its composition includes internet industry, child safety advocacy organisations, educational and civil liberties communities, government departments and law enforcement. In 2010 it published a report[7] recommending various strategies to promote online safety for young people through education and stated all stakeholders (parents, schools, government and industry) need to work collaboratively to improve cybersafety.

In 2009 the American Federal Communications Commission, the Federal Trade Commission and the Department of Education released *NetCetera*[8] which is a guide for parents to assist in speaking to their children about 'being online'. It identifies the online risks of texting, posting images or comments and provides the tools for parents to start the conversation with their children about the risks technology can bring.

The Children's Agenda for Digital Opportunity is an initiative by the Federal Communications Commission to inform parents and teachers about what it describes as 'four pillars' of technology use for young people:

- digital access;
- digital literacy;
- digital citizenship; and
- digital safety.

---

[5] UK Council for Child Internet Safety (2013).

[6] Childnet International (2013).

[7] Online Safety and Technology Working Group (2010).

[8] NetCetera (2013).

Wired Safety[9] is one of the world's largest internet safety and education resources. It collates a range of resources and information for young people and parents including:

- Wired Kids Inc;
- Wiredkids org;
- Cyber Law Enforcement Organisation Network;
- Stop Cyberbullying;
- Net bullies; and
- Teenangels.

Cybersmart![10] is another website developed to collate a range of initiatives including:

- online workshops for professional development of teachers and parents;
- student curriculum web-based tools for young people; and
- educator toolbar provides 24/7 access to resources.

5.1.3 *International Collaborations*

The need for international collaborations in dealing with cyberbullying and promoting best-practice programs and strategies is important. The internet has no borders, needs no entry visas or passports to enter into young people's homes. Single jurisdictions are no longer effective, stakeholder networks are increasingly important and international law is required to effectively investigate serious cyberbullying and cybercrime offences. Some key international arrangements currently exist.

United Nations Crime Prevention and Criminal Justice Commission focused on two themes at its 2011 session:

- the nature and scope of the problem of misuse of new technologies in the abuse and exploitation of children; and
- responses to the problem of the misuse of new technologies in the abuse and exploitation of children.

Council of Europe Convention on Cyber-crime is an international treaty on cybercrime. The Convention requires signatories to criminalise certain conduct and powers for law enforcement. The Convention is not limited to European nations and Australia has recently indicated a willingness to accede.

An international alliance of law enforcement agencies, the Virtual Global Taskforce, was launched in 2003. Partner countries include Australia, United

---

[9] Wired Safety (2013).

[10] Cybersmart! (2013).

States, Britain, Canada, Italy, New Zealand, United Arab Emirates and Interpol. Its main aim is to protect children from online abuse and exploitation.

The Australian/European Research Training School has been established to determine world's best-practice in developing researchers to work on the prevention and intervention of cyberbullying and benchmark these against international findings. In 2010 30 European and 18 Australian early career researchers and PhD candidates participated in a joint venture on cyberbullying research and related fields.

5.1.4 Professional Development

Teachers who are confident and familiar with technology and its uses will be equipped to support young people in developing strategies for online safety. Professional Development needs to address the attitudes and perceptions towards both offline and online bullying as well as the skills required to use the technology in effective teaching and learning programs. Perceptions from teachers about the use of Information Communications Technology (ICT) in the curriculum also needs to be addressed. Limited teacher competence and confidence in addition to resistance to change and negative attitudes amongst some are seem as barriers in the use of ICT. Many teachers site lack of time, limited availability to effective training, limited accessibility and technical support within the schools as barriers as well. Pre-service teacher education should include units or subjects on awareness and skills for preventing and managing both offline and online bullying. However, regular training and support to understand and respond appropriately to cyberbullying is paramount.

Dealing with the impacts of cyberbullying needs to take a socio-ecological perspective which includes an effective whole-school approach. An effective whole-school intervention program:

- is well planned;
- involves multiple stakeholders;
- includes students in program development and delivery;
- addresses multiple risk and protective factors;
- provides age-appropriate materials, discussions and time limits;
- creates a gender-specific approach;
- intervenes when target behaviour is emerging; and
- creates a long-term intervention.

Teachers can promote positive relationships by:

- establishing networks of buddies;
- establishing circles of support;
- creating peer mentors; and
- finding ways to highlight an individual students' talent.

Embedding cybersafety into the broader curriculum and encouraging pro-social behaviours as part of classroom management and how to respond to inappropriate internet use would also be important.

5.1.5 Cyberbullying and the Law

Excessive regulation of young people and the use of technology does not provide for the learning of the skills they need to function in the 'real-world' post school. Banning mobile phones from schools will not necessarily reduce the incidents of cyberbullying. We need to remember, cyberbullying is another form of bullying behaviour so focusing on the behaviours rather than the technology is key. Regulating technology or taking legal action will not change behaviours.

The law, as such, struggles to keep abreast of changes in new technologies and thereby cyberbullying. In Australia, bullying and cyberbullying are not criminal offences per se. The first case of cyberbullying to be brought to court in Australia was in 2010. The accused escaped a jail sentence, even though the person he had sent vicious text messages to committed suicide, he was found guilty of stalking. The law described the cyberbullying offence as 'Using a Carriage Service to Menace, Harass or Cause Offence'.

Another important aspect with criminalising cyberbullying is whether the person is deemed by the law to be responsible for their actions. Criminal responsibility is age determined, which in Australia, is 10 years. Therefore any child aged between 10 and 14 years may be criminally responsible for cyberbullying. Anyone over the age of 14 years is considered to have the capacity to be liable for their actions. Many police will question whether a foolish or childish act by a young person in these age brackets, who may lack empathy and impulse control, should warrant a criminal record which will impact on the remainder of their lives. The criminalisation of young people has attracted much debate. Education and counselling are viewed as more appropriate options when the motivation has been more about naïve experimentation or rule-breaking amongst adolescents.

Cyberbullying may include the following broad criminal offences:

- assaults;
- threats;
- extortion;
- stalking;
- harassment; and
- indecent conduct.

There is a raft of legislation on cyberstalking, misuse of telecommunication and harassment to criminalise these behaviours.

Telecommunications offences may also be relevant though more difficult to prove. Threats of violence communicated by mobile phone, text message or posted to a website may constitute a crime. If the individual believes the threat to be real it could be classified assault. For example, if a text message is send stating they will be bashed at break time. Compensation by the targets of cyberbullying through civil proceedings may be more successful as the case need only be proved on 'probabilities' rather than criminal standard. Age is also not a factor in civil law. However, this course of action is costly and time consuming and the target will need to restate the experience of cyberbullying. As cyberbullying has an impact on a young person's mental wellbeing, a target can claim based on intentional infliction of physical harm. Whilst some people who engage in cyberbullying believe they are 'having fun' or 'playing a joke', these actions have long-lasting consequences to those people they have targeted.

Invasion of privacy due to cyberbullying is also a criminal offence. Material and private information which is given widespread publicity online causes harm in the form of distress, embarrassment and/or humiliation. Uploading posts or images online via websites, chat rooms, blogs, wikis, bulletin boards which embarrass, humiliate or otherwise cause distress may have action for defamation. The person engaging in cyberbullying would need to have communicated to at least one person other than the target the defamatory material for it to be a crime and we know many young people forward on images or re post messages sent to them.

In 2013, in Australia the first national Bullying, Young People and the Law Symposium was conducted. This was attended by legal, law enforcement and educational experts throughout Australia and New Zealand and was a joint initiative between the Alannah and Madeline Foundation's National Centre Against Bullying and the Australian Federal Police. The Symposium recommend the following approach:

- education;
- appropriate responses by organisations to incidences of bullying and cyberbullying;
- the establishment of a national digital communication tribunal; and
- an appropriate legal framework to address bullying and cyberbullying.[11]

Schools have a well-established duty of care to their students and staff. This extends beyond reasonable precautions against physical injury and into psychological injury. Schools also have a duty to protect the student from the conduct of other students. Duty of care issues become more complicated in the context of cyberbullying as this form of bullying is beyond the temporal or geographical scope of the duty. Cyberbullying can and does occur 24/7, at home and on weekends. Schools' responsibility for cyberbullying and the potential criminal implications are not well understood. Schools are resorting to criminal law often from frustration, fear of litigation or in the interests of safety. The unrealistic fear of schools being sued is impeding their ability to respond to cyberbullying

---

[11] AMF (2013).

appropriately. In Australia parents are not generally legally liable for the acts of their children.

Cybersafety reflects legal issues and implications such as:

- balance between freedom of speech and the right to privacy;
- criminal charges against users;
- discrimination and vilification;
- civil claims against users;
- legislation controlling the behaviour of Internet Service Providers (ISPs); and
- responsibility and rights of the school in responding.[12]

A significant frustration for schools is the inability to trace the cyberbullying especially as the impact within the school community is evident. There is also the inability, even with the support of the police, to remove the inappropriate content from the website. Actions and information between schools, police and ISPs need to be more collaborative and timely.

Community education is one of the most important elements to prevent cyberbullying. Young people are not necessarily aware of the legal implications of cyberbullying. They view cyberbullying as it relates to student-student behaviour and not from a larger view. Many students may not be aware that they are engaging in cyberbullying and that it may also be against the law.

5.1.6 Cyberbullying of Teachers

Cyberbullying directed towards teachers is increasing due to the anonymity of some online sites. Individual staff members or even the school itself can be the target of inappropriate content. Social networking sites and the 'rate my teacher' site has seen many 'attacks' on teachers by students which not only has a professional impact but also impacts on the teacher personally. There is limited success by schools and teachers in removing comments from these sites. Students have also been known to upload videos secretly filmed at school on mobile phones to internet video sharing sites and accompany them with inappropriate comments. The number of false and defamatory comments made online by students is increasing, some even falsely accusing teachers of being paedophiles or engaging in other criminal activities, posting personal details such as addresses or setting up false profiles on 'dating' sites.

When developing policies and procedures in schools, cyberbullying of staff should also be recognised. In addition the ethical and legal issues provide concern for teachers as there is limited clarity on the legal requirements and implications of cyberbullying. Young people are quite savvy and are able to post defamatory or negative comments without actually crossing the point where legal action could be

---

[12] McGrath (2009).

taken. The relationships between students and teachers are sometimes fluid as some younger teachers do not understand the possible implications of sending a student a text message for example. As we need to teach young people about their digital reputation, perhaps we also need to extend this awareness into pre-service teacher education.

References

Alannah and Madeline Foundation (2013). Retrieved July 24, 2013, from http://www.amf.org.au/bypalrecommendations.

Childnet International (2013). Retrieved July 27, 2013, from http://www.childnet.com/resources.

Childnet International (2013). *Know it All.* Retrieved July 27, 2013, from http://www.childnet.com/resources/kia.

Cross, D., Shaw, T., Hearn, L., Epstein, M., Monks, H., Lester, L., et al. (2009). *Australian Covert Bullying Prevalence Study (ACBPS), Child Health Promotion Research Centre.* Perth: Edith Cowan University, Retrieved May 4, 2013, from www.deewr.gov.au/Schooling/NationalSafeSchools/Pages/research.aspx.

Cybersmart! (2013). Retrieved July 27, 2013, from http://cybersmart.org.

McGrath, H. (2009). *Young People and Technology:A review of the current literature.* (2nd ed.). South Melbourne, Vic: The Alannah and Madeline Foundation.

National Telecommunications and Information Administration USA (2010). *Youth Safety on a Living Internet: Report of the Online Safety and Technology Working Group.* Retrieved July 27, 2013, from http://www.ntia.doc.gov/legacy/reports/2010/OSTWG_Final_Report_060410.pdf?

NetCetera (2013). *Chatting with kids about being online.* Retrieved July 27, 2013, from http://www.onguardonline.gov/articles/pdf-0001.pdf.

ThinkUKnow (2013). Retrieved July 27, 2013, from http://www.thinkyouknow.co.uk.

UK Council for Child Internet Safety Updated (2010). *Good Practice Guidance for the Providers of Social Networking and Other User Interactive Services.* Retrieved July 27, 2013, from http://dera.ioe.ac.uk/1970/3/industry%20guidance%20%20%20social%20networking.pdf.

UK Council for Child Internet Safety (2013). *Click Clever Click Safe.* Retrieved July 27, 2013, from http://www.nidirect.gov.uk/click-clever-click-safe.

Wired Safety (2013). Retrieved July 27, 2013, from https://www.wiredsafety.org.